DON'T STOP, WON'T STOP

A 5-STEP SYSTEM TO FINDING YOUR PASSION,
PERSONALITY AND PURPOSE. HELP FILL THE
EMPTY VOID IN WHAT YOU CALL LIFE

ALEC MOONEE

CONTENTS

15 QUESTIONS YOU MUST ASK YOURSELF

(OPEN YOUR MIND TO FIND THE OPPORTUNITY)

Don't Stop, Won't Stop

15 QUESTIONS YOU MUST ASK YOURSELF.

www.AlecMoonee.com

These Worksheet Includes:

- 15 Questions you cannot leave unanswered.
- 15 Deep thinking questions to unpack your passion.
- The ability to open your mind.

The last thing we want is you not having the head start to finding your meaning, purpose, passion.

To receive your 15 Question Worksheet, Visit this link (PS. It's Free):

https://tinyurl.com/DontStopWontStop

INTRODUCTION

"The mystery of human existence lies not in just staying alive, but in finding something to live for."

— *FYODOR DOSTOYEVSKY*

There are well over seven billion lives in existence. Each one of them is preoccupied with one thing or another. There are those who are struggling to keep their bellies filled, and then there are those who are pursuing wealth beyond imagination. Some long for love while others wait for something magical to happen. Every soul has a story, and every person exists for a reason.

Lately, it seems like our reason for existence is only to earn money so that we can pay our dues such as taxes and utility bills. It is quite a depressing realization, and it is completely wrong as well.

Our purpose in life is far greater. The only reason we feel this way is because we either start comparing our situation to someone else and feel we will never be able to be as good as them, or we never really pay attention to what we could become because the unknown always frightens us. It is this fear of the unknown that has kept us at bay, limited our vision and, dare I say, it has cast a shadow of doubt on our own capabilities.

Every time I ask someone if they would like to do something else that would actually make them happy, most replied that they cannot. When asked why, they stated the obvious fear of losing their primary source of income if they even tried to pursue something else.

Do not get me wrong, I am not here to tell you that you should quit your job right away and you will find something far better instantly. If only life was that simple, I would perhaps be on a remote exotic island of my own, ripping right through the blue waters of the open sea without a care in the world in my luxury yacht. I am, however, here to incept an idea that may sound familiar, but would change everything for you if you truly pursued that instead.

Life is a gift, and we only live once. The problem is we do not come with an expiration date either, and that is a big problem. We keep on pushing things to "some other day" without ever realizing that we may never get to see that other day. We are so caught up in a system that has been designed to pay us a miser sum in exchange for sacrificing our passion, our dreams, and our untapped potential. We continue to function as a small cog in a giant machine, and we are doing exactly what the curators and operators want us to do.

You wake up every day, get ready, and leave for work. You spend hours there doing something that clearly is exhausting so that you can get a paycheck at the end of the month which clearly makes you feel underpaid. You come home, all broken and tired, and there is a pile of bills ready to devour that hard-earned money. Perhaps the TV might have something to cheer you up. A quick glance at the channels and nothing except news of global crisis, financial downfalls, and calamity all around.

You eventually get up, fix yourself a dinner, eat, and go off to sleep. The next day, the cycle repeats. It has been going on like this for years now, and guess what? I see the same happening for years to come. Ask yourself one simple question:

"Is this what you call life?"

The short version of the answer is no. This mere existence for a purpose that is serving someone else, who one day would say goodbye to you and hire someone else. All those bills and taxes will keep coming too. You have done well to satisfy the authorities, but who is looking after what you desire, what you want, and what you wish to do? The only person who can truly understand you is YOU!

The problem is not life, but the purpose that we attach to it. We are born with abilities, talents, and the capability to pursue far more than just a job that pays you some sum. The minute you take part in this rat race, you are sidelining your purpose indefinitely.

Everyone wishes to do something in their life that would make life itself worth living. Jobs and businesses are a small part, but the minute you prioritize those above your own self, you stop living life.

An astounding four of every 10 Americans claim that their life has no clear purpose (Cooper, 2016). They have no idea what they would want to do if even the slightest change was to come their way. To them, life starts and quite literally ends at work. Their social life, their friends, and their loved ones suffer as a result, and there is no one else to be blamed here either.

We lead our lives through the choices we make. I have

seen millionaires who cannot get a good night's sleep nor are able to enjoy a laugh or two, or even take some time off to enjoy life itself. This is an eye-opener for anyone who thinks money is the solution. I assure you, it is not. These millionaires created their own purpose and that was to ensure they could earn more, thus sacrificing their relationships, their social activities, their own interests, and everything in between.

If you have been feeling down lately, found yourself lost in your thoughts, daydreaming about what life could have been, and where it all went wrong, it is time to find that missing spark in life and start living. The journey will not be easy, but I assure you, it will be well worth it.

WHY SHOULD YOU READ THIS BOOK?

Life is nothing short of a mystery. Only a select few actually dare to solve the riddle and find a purpose to live while the rest of us toil away in a robotic, monotonous and frankly purposeless existence. We choose that lifestyle in hopes of achieving true happiness, but let me be the first to say that happiness does not come without meaning. With a certain meaning that we latch on to, we can certainly acquire happiness, but it just does not work the other way around.

There is a reason why children always seem to be having a great time, regardless of their fame or fortunes, and that has everything to do with the fact that they act, not think. We, on the other hand, magically grow up and are led to believe that we should think before we act to pursue something that may genuinely make us feel happy, alive, and joyful. We are far too busy thinking about the consequences and those "what if?" questions.

If we magically acquire some free time from our chores and professional lives, we tend to waste it all away spying on what's going on with someone we may have never even met, using social media. Others prefer binge-watching their favorite TV shows on Netflix and other streaming platforms. I do enjoy a good movie or two, but that is not how I intend to waste my time at all. I would rather do something productive, something that would instill a sense of fulfillment, a liberating feeling of actually achieving something good and new.

If you are one of those who keeps on wondering how on earth a friend of yours is leading a terrific life, enjoying parties, hanging out with friends, and doing exactly the same job as you, the answer is just around the corner. All you need is a bit of a wake-up call.

I decided to write this book to address everyone who has felt lost, miserable, and hopeless. To anyone who seems to have lost a purpose and a meaning to life, it is never too late to rediscover yourself. By the end of this book, you too will learn just how the seemingly impossible can magically become possible. Before you know it, you will come out of your existence and start re-living life just the way you had always wanted.

What Makes Me An Authority?

This certainly calls for a quick introduction of mine. After all, you cannot go on believing the words of a complete stranger unless that stranger holds something unique and definitive that would help establish some trust.

My name is Alec Moonee, and for anyone who may not know me, I am a motivational speaker. I am passionate about what I do, and to ensure that I do it right, I always carry out my research and ensure I have all the evidence and statistics to support my ideas. There is no point in telling someone that they can do something no one has ever done before without providing some form of proof or evidence to suggest the notion is even possible. However, I know of people who have changed their lives and gone on to become success stories in their own rights. Right about now, it would be fair to confess that I was not always a motivational speaker myself. I too needed a wake-up call.

Not long ago, I was involved in a horrific and life-altering car crash. It was just after my 26th birthday, and lucky enough, I lived to see another day. As I was recovering, I had nothing but time to reflect back on what I had done so far. I was in for a shock of a lifetime to figure out I was not going anywhere with my life. I had no clear purpose, I definitely did not inherit a fortune and neither was I able to find something important to stick to in life. It was a very harsh reality, one that I was living without realizing how lost I was.

Soon afterward, I recovered and my physiotherapy sessions ended. I eventually went on to obtain a degree in communication from the University of Southern California. I always had a thing for public speaking, and this degree prepared me further for it. I now had everything I needed to seek and establish a career out of public speaking.

Fast forward to today, I organize various public speaking events and webinars where I meet with some of the finest people on earth, motivate them to redefine their lives, and rediscover their purposes. I have already authored the book *Brain F**k*, and now you are reading the second one *Don't Stop, Won't Stop*, both of which talk about the psychology of human beings and how easily they get distracted from the real purpose of life and become just another number for banks, institutions, and statistics. Both these books focus on how one can lead a much happier life, one that always seems to be fulfilled and satisfactory. The bonus is, you do not need to belong to a certain walk of life. Take the knowledge and apply it wherever you may be, whatever you may be doing, and see the results of your efforts take shape.

The real strength lies in your own self; it is the dedication that you bring to the table. With that said, it is time for us to start our journey and rediscover a life we seem to have lost along the way.

"I don't stop, and I won't stop until I acquire what is rightfully mine; life!" - Alec Moonee

"People often say that this or that person has not yet found himself.

But the self is not something one finds, it is something one creates."

— THOMAS SZASZ

STOP EXISTING - START LIVING: HERE'S HOW

Take a seat. Relax and take a few good and deep breaths to help calm your nerves. You have had a very long day at work, or you are just fed up with this pointless existence that is serving you with nothing but more agony. You are not alone in this.

For centuries, people have felt the same, and it only took a few days for them to crack out of their existence and jump onto the right track. If they could have done it centuries ago, we would be a more advanced civilization. Surely, we stand a far better chance at this than they did. Our probability of success is much higher. The real question is, how? How do you do that despite having all the knowledge in the world at your fingertips? How can you actually go on to change your life?

For that, we first need to analyze where we are at this point in time.

Once you have calmed down and removed every unnecessary thought from your mind, I want you to picture yourself on the yellow sands of an exotic beach. The crystal clear blue waters of the ocean seem to stretch on forever and continue to crash merely a few yards away from you. Listen to the sound of the waves. Smell that fresh air blowing across your face. The sun is merciful and the wind is just right. It is neither warm nor cold. A perfect setting for you to take a dive or surf, or even paraglide if you are into some adrenaline-pumping sports. The world is yours, and you get to do whatever you please.

It feels nice, doesn't it? That is just a mere glimpse of what life is. That is hardly a fraction of what you can feel like if you truly start living your life. Remove what you see on the TV, remove your concept of financial gains, and eight to nine figures in the bank. I assure you, money can never buy you happiness.

"I hope everybody could get rich and famous and will have everything they ever dreamed of, so they will know that it's not the answer."

— *JIM CARREY*

The man behind some of the finest movies of our time, Jim Carrey. For him to say such a thing, it certainly hits us hard. For us regular people, who often go on to fantasize about all that money and fame, this is a knockout punch. If money isn't the answer, what is?

KNOWING THE DIFFERENCE

One fine day, I decided to ask random people about the difference between existing and living. I was surprised to see that a sweeping majority had no clue of how these are any different. I do not blame them at all as there is a good chance they never came across such a question before.

There is a massive difference between existing and actually living life to the fullest. The first step of our journey starts with a huge barrier; one that we need to understand and resolve right away if we are to proceed any further.

Existence is just the biological presence of a being. Everything you see around you is a sign of existence. The trees, the birds, the animals, even the microscopic beings, all of them merely exist without serving much of a purpose or ever getting to live life the way they want to. Most lead their lives surviving, and that is where we are no different. We have come to terms with life as a period of time that we need to go through and survive. Truth be told, most of us are already doing the best we can. Think about it for a second. If you are able to provide for yourself, eat, sleep, and drink without an issue, why remain in this zone where we still continue to struggle? Can we not change a few things about life and come out of this biological presence? Can we not do something that would bring a more purposeful meaning to our life? We most certainly can.

To you, you may already be living a life, but if you are not able to squeeze time for yourself, for your loved ones, be able to socialize, be able to finish that project in your garage that has been gathering dust for the past 10 years, you aren't living life at all. You are just caught up in an endless loop that leads you nowhere.

You would know if you were living life to the fullest because every night, you would go to sleep knowing you lived your day to the max, and that you are eager to welcome tomorrow. You would know if you are doing it right because your relationship stands strong and there is not a shred of worry around you. Your neighbors would love to invite you over for dinner because they would be looking up to you, asking for your guidance to help them lead a life like yours. The best part is that when you help them out, your meaning of existence grows stronger, and in comes a barrage of happiness and joy.

Leading a life that is more like that of a robot, performing functions like you are taken over by some autopilot command, that may be okay for a week or two. Soon, you would feel something missing. With the passage of time, everything would start to annoy you, and you would surround yourself with so much negativity that even the simplest pleasures in life would feel like a burden on you.

You have the skills and the capabilities, and you know them fully well, yet you are so caught up in your regular activities that you hardly pay them any attention. You are least bothered to put in any effort or to be a little creative because it seems pointless. These are all symptoms to make you realize that you are just existing, and such actions are pushing you away from life itself.

On the polar opposite end, you have this person who works the regular nine to five job, but clearly he is doing something that allows him to always smile and take up challenges with ease. He is never stressed, enjoys a healthy life, has a great relationship going on, goes on vacations, and is even learning new skills and practicing new hobbies. Everyone in the office envies him. There is always such a person within workplaces, and everyone would know of them not because this person wants the attention, but because everyone can simply not ignore them.

I am sure we all want to be like that person. We all want to lead our lives on our terms. Putting the obvious bills and taxes aside, we want to have a life of our own away from work and the stresses that follow.

The reason why such personalities are rare to find has everything to do with our choices. What we have or what we do not have somehow has everything to do with the way we look at life and the efforts we put in to make it better. Most of us fail on that front drastically, and we might not even realize it. The others, those who somehow muster the courage to make a difference for themselves, are clearly putting in their heart and soul in pursuing a purpose.

These people, if you observe them closely, follow certain rules in life which they set for themselves and abide by till the end. Their consistency is the key which we clearly lack. The minute we believe we have found a better opportunity, we do not hesitate to jump and grab it. In the process, we are letting go of all those years of work and any reputation that we may have built, and we push ourselves to start all over again. Yes, the opportunity may be paying you a little more, but it may also be taking away far too much from us.

Instead of jumping ship, here's a better way to go about it. Let us take small steps, one at a time, and change our current way of living into one that we would never wish to let go of. Let us make this journey into a phase of life where every small achievement is felt and appreciated by our inner being, and by the people we care about. You will soon see a difference, and a significant one at that.

For us to take such small steps, let us go through some of the most common symptoms to look out for and identify which ones we are experiencing Even if you end up relating to only one of these, your life currently is at a standstill.

"Knowing is half the battle."

For this to work for you, you need to ensure you are honest with yourself. I know, we generally loathe the idea of criticizing ourselves and pointing out our own mistakes. However, to really proceed forward, we need to ensure utmost honesty, even if that sounds a little harsh.

1. You wake up every day, and every time you continue to ponder just how bland, monotonous, and boring your next nine to ten hours are going to be. Just the mere thought of

work makes you want to go back to bed. Meeting the same faces, doing the same tasks over and over again, maneuvering through the rush hour traffic and not to forget the hassle of finding a decent parking spot. Everything about it seems off, yet you cannot pick up the phone and call it in sick because you have already done that a few weeks ago.

2. Whether at work, in a meeting, or even at home, you often start daydreaming about how life could have been different. Perhaps you wanted to be a musician and compose songs. Maybe you were interested in pursuing a career in the gaming industry and wanted to create genuinely entertaining games. Perhaps you just wanted a vacation but either the work keeps you from taking one, or your finances are depleting faster than you can save. While you daydream, a lot happens around you, and there is a significant chance you might miss out on something important. That might lead you to issues that you would later have to deal with.

3. Every now and then, you find yourself lost in your own little world. Everyone around you seems to talk about how they see their next five years, and what they would be doing to ensure their goals are met. In the meantime, you

STOP EXISTING - START LIVING: HERE'S HOW | 27

continue to show interest despite knowing you not really thought about the next year, let alone five years of time. You feel depressed, embarrassed, confused and utterly lost.

4. Every day, you spend hours and hours going through YouTube or Netflix browsing through the endless list of content and shows. You have already spent hundreds of hours watching most of them and yet you still continue doing the same. You do this at work, at home, and even during social gatherings when possible. All that time which could have been used productively, gone. The only way you can comfort yourself is by rationalizing just how you had nothing more to do.

5. You do not plan for what to expect and prepare for it. You feel you are better at being the kind of person who handles the situation as it arrives. You find it cumbersome to actually prepare yourself for something that apparently would not happen. You never really plan ahead until you arrive at a point and realize you are not at all prepared to handle the situation. You do not find yourself proactively coping and making the most of what life has to offer.

6. A new opportunity comes knocking on your door, and everything sounds interesting. The

second you realize it requires a little more work than you normally prefer doing, you throw it right out the window and hope a better opportunity will come by soon.

7. You value your comfort zone over everything. You cannot be bothered to go out and jog early in the morning, you cannot go to sleep without watching a movie, and you cannot go to do groceries because the superstore is a mile away. You find it exhausting just thinking about it.

8. You find flaws in everyone and everything. Negativity takes over you and you start criticizing important things in your life, including people and relationships.

9. You feel like, despite all the effort you put in and all the hard work you do, you still fail to make an impression. You feel like you will never be able to make a difference and be accepted as someone who deserves praise and appreciation.

I will give you a minute to go through the list once again. This time, close your eyes and try to see if any of these spark something. If you feel a connection to any of these, or if you can relate to any of these nine points, you are merely existing.

Once again, it is hard to accept the cold and hard truth. The fact of the matter, however, is that you are doing something wrong which is leading you into such a state. It is never late to stop, think, and recalibrate your direction. It is never too late to realize you are wrong and that you wish to make things right. The only person who will be affected directly by these changes is you.

I have given you a list of symptoms to relate to, just to figure out if you are stuck in a state of existence. Let me now introduce you to how it would be like if you were to fully understand the concept of living and actually start living your life to the fullest. This would further clarify the difference between the two.

The day you start living life to the fullest, and you find your purpose:

- You will be able to focus primarily on things that would allow you to attain personal growth. You would be able to focus on things that would truly make you happy and provide you with a sense of accomplishment.
- Your worries, your sorrows, doubts, questions, and that void of feeling hopelessness would just disappear instantly. Why? Because you would know the exact reason for your existence and

you would have found yourself a purpose to actually stick to.

- You will eventually start living life on your own terms. No longer will you have to follow societal norms and traits blindly. You will no longer feel pressured by your peers or the expectations that others have for you. You will be leading a far better lifestyle.

- Knowing every day is a gift, being thankful, and measuring your success through the small achievements, you will always find peace, and your stress would be overpowered by sheer joy and satisfaction.

- You will now be in control of everything that goes on in your life. You will no longer be fearing the possible circumstances to determine or influence your choices in life.

Quite an exciting future, don't you think? It is definitely a lot better than the current state of mere existence we find ourselves in. Let me be the first one to tell you that you have everything you need to get started. Yes, you may need help in getting there, which is why I have carefully planned the next five chapters as your five essential steps to help you get to your destination.

From here on out, I want you to promise yourself that:

- You will truly remain honest with yourself.
- You will do whatever is necessary to change your life for the better.
- You will never let external pressure mislead you into making the wrong choices.
- You will never fall back to your old habits.
- You will put your heart and soul in ensuring you make things right.
- You will pursue whatever your purpose may be, to the maximum of your capabilities.
- You will always keep an open mind.

That is basically all you need before you take your first step.

THE FIRST STEP

"A journey of a thousand miles starts with a first step."

Take the first step and you will already be one step closer to realizing your dream. Keep that motivation high and believe in yourself. We will need both of these throughout the book to acquire the results we want.

You do not have to go through a horrific tragedy or an accident like I did, just to get that wake-up call. You do not need to put yourself through misery. All you need is determination and will. Here's an eye-opener for you: if you are reading this line, you have already proven that you have the strength, the courage, the will, and the desire to change.

I officially welcome you to the first hour of a new life. A life that you will go on to live and enjoy for the rest of your days. Without wasting any more time, let us dive into our first step and discover just how we can find and identify our passion and our purpose in life. We will go through what keeps us from exploring our desires and how we can overcome these barriers to truly start living life.

To further assist you, I would recommend keeping a notebook and a pen handy. You may need to note down some important aspects which you could refer to quickly. This is actually a good habit to get into. You never know when you may need to refer to such notes in the future. The notepad also helps you to brainstorm and write various points that may help you further clarify the situation and ideas as we shall discuss in the next chapter.

"Not until we are lost do we begin to understand ourselves."

— HENRY DAVID THOREAU

STEP 1 - HOW TO LIVE A LIFE FILLED WITH PASSION?

Welcome to the first of the five steps that the program in this book offers. You have already shown your determination by going through the previous chapter, and so far, you are doing brilliantly.

The first step of our program is all about our inner selves, and how we can discover our passions and purposes. For us to really pursue these, there are a few things we should address first. These are some of the most common issues of life. In fact, these are so common that we quite literally overlook them most of the time. Just because we ignore them does not mean they do not exist. They most certainly do.

These are a number of factors that influence our lifestyle choices, push us to a zone where we end up sacrificing the most just to please others. So many great talents that could have made it big gave up chasing their dream because whatever they wanted to pursue, whatever their passion was, they just couldn't impress others.

How many times have you decided to do something and then immediately decided to retreat because of irrational fears, or because of what your peers, friends, and family members will have to say about it? How many times have you felt you may be on to something big, but then a discussion or two later, you had to let it go with a heavy heart? We have all been there. It hurts and it hinders us mentally. We may never be able to think of something similar ever again, not because we don't want to, but because we would be too afraid of how others would react to our choices. This is exactly the kind of thing that stands as a massive barrier between you and a life filled with passion and purpose.

In this chapter, we will explore what are these factors and how each of them affects us and our abilities. We will dive further to see if it is possible to overcome these, and if so, how. We will eventually learn some great tips which can help us take this first step towards a better life ahead. So much to learn, so much to explore. Ensure that your notepad is ready because I will encourage you to write down a few things and later review the same to see how we can help ourselves from our current situation.

THE INVISIBLE BARRIERS

Friends, family, peers, colleagues: they all play a part in our lives. They all contribute to our lives in one way or another, whether we give them credit or not. However, one thing that most of us tend to forget is that they too are human beings, just like us. There are times they may feel frustrated or jealous, and at times they may just be plainly ignorant. Human beings make mistakes, and there is nothing we can do about it but identify these errors and ensure we keep our distance from potential consequences these mistakes can bring forth.

You might be wondering, why on earth am I talking about these 'factors' and where exactly am I going with this, right? The point I am trying to make here is quite simple; for anyone to proceed with our journey, we must first understand, identify and realize what exactly is it that holds us back from pursuing a better life. As I mentioned earlier, there are not one but numerous factors that come into play. Some of these have to do with your own fears and phobias while others have to do with the people you interact with.

In one way or another, these factors, as long as they

remain, will never allow us to live properly. They will always find a way to get back in, influence our choices, and alter the course of our life. However, that does not mean that we cannot learn how to counter these influences.

To begin with, we will start exploring our own psychological issues. You may be suffering from low-confidence or low self-esteem, but the number one issue people face these days is fear.

Fear

Just like the feeling of happiness, joy, or sadness, we experience fear as well. Fear, in the simplest form, is essentially an emotion that is induced by perceived danger or threat. When faced with such a situation, our body experiences physiological changes, most of which take place immediately. These will lead to some massive behavioral changes.

To state an example of how quickly these changes occur and how our behavior changes, let us explore the possible situation of facing a spider. You would be in your own state of mind, doing something and feeling focused, when all of a sudden you are presented with this eerie, multi-legged creature crawling towards you. Within a split second, your mind perceives it as a danger or a possible threat, and the fear effect kicks in. Your mood changes, your reflexes take over your body, you jump on a chair or the bed, or you just scream and leave the room altogether to feel safe.

So much happens in just a split second, and you quite literally have no control over your thoughts, your mind, and your body. You just go with the flow and let your body decide what to do next.

On the other hand, there are those who are not scared by spiders in the least. These people would probably laugh, go into the room, and just scare the spider away. Mind you, this is the very same spider that almost gave you a heart attack. Why do you think that happens? The entire issue lies in the definition of the word **fear**.

I used the words 'perceived threat' earlier on, and I did that on purpose. Whatever we perceive does not necessarily label this thing as such. If a spider is scary for you, it may not be scary for me at all. It is just a difference in perspectives. This may have something to do with your past experiences, which we will discuss later on, or this may just be because you have no idea what a spider does and why.

The biggest fear, however, is not of animals or things at all. It is not even the intimidating boss in the office or the creepy neighbor either. The biggest fear is fear of the unknown. It is human nature that they will fear whatever they do not know.

Imagine driving down a road that has no street lights for miles. You are the only person driving there that night and you are alone. After a while, you arrive at a crossing and every direction is dark. Unless you already know where you wish to go, there is a great chance you might turn back. This is natural because we have no idea what we can expect if we are to take any other road and continue on. We could be a victim of theft, robbery, or worse even, alien abduction! When you start letting fear control you, all kinds of irrational thoughts start popping up. This would then impair your progress and push you back into retreat.

Our lives work in quite a similar fashion. When we decide to launch a small business, invest in stocks, or do anything that may have a significant impact on our lives, we start focusing more on the unknown. Instead of planning, we may start giving in to the fear and eventually retreat. At the same time, someone else decided to take a shot and actually made it big. In the end, we would continue to curse ourselves for being afraid when there was never anything to be afraid of.

For us to pursue our passion, we must first learn how to overlook our fears. Fearing the unknown is perhaps the biggest reason why so many of us do not end up successful. Those who have made it looked at fear as an opportunity to explore and learn from. They were able to go past their fears, understand what they needed to be careful of and how they could avoid getting themselves in hot water. To think of some notable examples, Mark Zuckerberg created Facebook, while Elon Musk went on to establish a multi-billion dollar empire with Tesla, and that is just in our times. Hundreds of thousands of such names exist in the history books.

All of these successful people ensured a few things:

- They never feared the unknown.
- They always had a plan.
- They stuck to their routines.
- They worked smart, not hard.
- They grabbed every opportunity, big or small.
- They always moved forward and never looked back.

We are virtually doing the polar opposite of all that, and everything I mentioned above has to do with our fear of the unknown. How? Let's take a closer look.

If I was to tell you to start waking up bright and early, go out for a good running session, eat healthy, and do other healthy activities throughout the day, what would be your first thought?

"Too much hassle!"

Exactly. That is where we are wrong. The reason is that we are far too comfortable in being lazy and sticking to our current habits, and we fear we may have to do a lot more work in order to create a new routine, let alone maintain it. Those who have managed to get their routine in order go on to actually enjoy the routine itself. It may not be satisfactory or the most amazing routine on earth, but it will certainly bring your comfort levels up.

By maintaining a healthy routine, you will be able to wake up early and get a head-start on things. You will be able to eat healthy and maintain a well-balanced diet, with all the goodness that brings you. Your physique would improve and so would your stamina, and we all know how important that is, don't we?

You will also be able to feel full of energy and fresh wherever you go. The more energy you have, the more you will be able to focus. The better you focus, the better you perform. And finally, when you come home, you will be able to rest well too.

Frankly, I do not see any downside to that, do you? I do not see why people are so confused and fearful of changing their old habits and adopting a healthier way of living. That is just one aspect, but an important one that we need to work on.

When in a routine, you will automatically be able to perform better and thus allow more opportunities to come your way. It could be a promotion at work, it could be a new relationship in sight or even a potential job offer from another employer altogether. Anything can happen as long as you put your heart and soul into doing something good for your own self.

When an opportunity does come by, do not wait. Grab it and move on. As long as it is not depreciating your financial gains, there is no reason to hold back. If the opportunity requires you to switch careers, rest assured the new employer saw something in you and they know you can do this. If they know, you should too. Grab it and take this as an opportunity to learn something completely new and unique. Failure is definitely a possibility, but treat it as nothing more than a rare chance. Do not ruminate on it. Focus more on the great possibilities of meeting new and exciting team members, a great working environment, and to earn possible promotions that may just pay you rather well.

The fear of failure is quite a real thing, but it is only as real as you make it. If you were to walk on a thin edge and continue fearing that you might fall off, chances are you actually will. Instead, what if you started telling yourself that you have got this and that you can do it? Chances you will actually end up doing it.

If you fear something, look at the opposite possibility. If you fear that you might fail, you can always feel excited knowing that you can also succeed. If you fear you might not be a good fit for an opportunity, tell yourself that you may just find some new hidden talent in you that would make you an ideal fit. It is that simple, yet we are not taught how to do that in our schools. We have to learn a few things the hard way.

According to SmallBizTrends, a jaw-dropping 33% of people in the US alone claim that the fear of failure is what holds them back from starting their own business ventures (Guta, 2018). That is a staggering number considering that the US is known as the land of opportunities.

When it comes to failure, here's a quick insight into one of the biggest success stories of our time. You may have heard of Dyson Ltd. This company was founded by Sir James Dyson. Before becoming a multi-billionaire, he spent all his savings into 5127 prototypes before coming up with the eponymous bagless vacuum machine. If anyone knows how to rule above fear, it is this person. He could have given up due to fear of failing on the first attempt, the 10th, the 100th, or even the 5126th attempt, but he refused to give into the idea of fearing failure. He knew he was onto something that would revolutionize everything, and guess what? It took him just one more attempt and then he cracked the code.

"The key to success is failure... Success is made up of 99 percent failure"

— *SIR JAMES DYSON*

Just like Jim Carrey, such a quote coming from the great Sir Dyson is quite a statement. If people as successful as he failed and learned from their failures; we should draw inspiration from the fact that failure is just a phase through which we learn and do even better. There is no reason for anyone to fear failure. It is through failure that we learn some of the most valuable aspects of life. Even babies fall and stumble a few times before they eventually understand, learn, and start to walk.

Do not let fear control you. You control your fears, and you decide what needs to be done and how. With fear in mind, we can never really move forward and hence we stick to the life we are accustomed to, as opposed to a life that could be far better and more joyful. Take risks and learn from failure. The only way to go is up.

Low Self-Confidence

This may sound a lot like fear, but the fact is that fear and low self-confidence are connected in a different way. It is through a low self-confidence that fear finds a room to enter your mind. If you are self-confident, fear would never have a room at the inn.

Here is a little exercise I have for you. For the next five minutes, put this book aside and start writing down what you feel is missing or wrong in your physical appearance and personality. Through this exercise, you will come to know exactly what causes you to have low self-confidence. By knowing your perceived flaws, you will be able to get a clear direction and know what it is you need to work on in order to be more self-confident.

There is always a phase in life where everyone feels as if they may be lacking self-confidence. They may not feel good about themselves or how they look, what they wear, and the list just goes on. However, when self-esteem is at an all-time low, and that feeling is prolonged, it can certainly bring forth some medical and psychological complications which can have long-lasting effects.

Self-confidence and self-esteem are the opinions people have about themselves. It is generally observed that a person who maintains healthy self-esteem would normally have this incredible positive vibe around them. They would feel positive, and their attitude would speak of nothing but positivity. This same principle is applied to their day to day life, where everything would go their way and all would be well.

On the other hand, there are those who suffer from a lack of self-confidence and self-esteem. These are the people who would always feel helpless and negative about everything in life. Due to the lack of self-confidence, they would not mingle in social gatherings, and they would shy away from opportunities that they could otherwise stand up and grab on to. They would feel left out and feel like a social outcast.

Low self-esteem and confidence may be a product of childhood issues and traumas one may have faced. While growing up, a child acquires knowledge quickly and when exposed to situations where they are being ridiculed or laughed at, most respond by lowering their self-esteem and hide. Once they grow up, it becomes a part of their personality. The good news is that the damage is not as bad as you might imagine. You can still change that.

School day memories are not the only things that either

give us the boost we need or push us towards the downfall we are trying to avoid. There are many other sources through which even adults get affected. These include our teachers, our siblings, our friends, our parents, and even the good old television. Messages from these sources can either praise us and bring our confidence all the way to 11, or they can continue to mock us and push us back to one.

Television, social media, and digital marketing in general are at play too. The messages we receive influence our self-confidence in more ways than one. What really hurts is that they use our vulnerabilities to promote their products. This means that if you wish to attend a high-profile party, you would not have any other option but to go for a very expensive perfume, an equally priced pair of shoes, a tuxedo from the finest selection and hundreds of dollars worth of hair products and lotions before you start feeling confident.

Millions of men are led to believe that their intimate moments can further be enhanced by buying products that would either prolong their sessions or give them unusual growth, and the constant push has led these men to feel insecure and low on confidence. Their opinions about themselves changed and they started doubting their own capabilities. The end result is anybody's guess.

The trouble is that it is not just products and the endless marketing campaigns that change our level of self-esteem, there are a few other ways through which we end up losing our confidence.

People are quick to tie expectations to others. You would always have at least one soul who would be expecting something out of you. The minute you start failing, you will constantly be reminded that you are letting them down. You may be trying your best to do something you know you cannot do, but it would never be enough.

"You cannot teach a fish how to fly."

If you were to start expecting a fish to fly, you would always be criticizing the fish. The reality is that a fish is not designed to fly, just as we might not be designed to do a certain task. If your interest and passion are not aligned, you would always struggle to do even the simplest of tasks.

By doing things you really do not wish to do or find unproductive, you will be back where you started from; an endless loop of meaningless work, without purpose or passion.

The other aspect of low self-confidence and self-esteem can also be attributed to our own expectations. You would certainly have some expectations of your own as well. The trouble is, we often believe that we are capable of doing a little more than possible and end up with extremely high expectations of ourselves. When we fail to live up to those expectations, our ego, our confidence, and our self-esteem all come crashing down.

It is indeed necessary to always know what you are asking of yourself. Always set achievable expectations. Start with smaller tasks and expectations. Once you start achieving them, mark them off your list and set something a little higher. Soon, you would know where your limit lies. By such time, you would have already improved your self-confidence and self-esteem to a new level, and everything would now seem a lot easier.

These are the only two sides, and our job is to pick one. No one wishes to pick the latter, and rightly so. No one wishes to find themselves in awkward positions where they are unable to communicate freely, interact with interesting people, take up opportunities, and lead a good life. The bad news is that while all of us want the brighter side, only a few of us actually put in the efforts required to bring their self-esteem and confidence up.

It takes commitment and dedication in order for us to realize our limits, know what we can do and what we cannot do. With self-confidence, you can pursue your goals with ease and continue on the path of success. Without it, you would never feel significant enough to pursue something meaningful, something you are passionate about, and worst of all, you would never be able to say 'no' to anyone. This means you will always be burdened by work and tasks, and that burden would never let you breathe freely, nor decide what you wish to do.

Prolonging your low self-esteem would push you to avoid matters as a coping habit (*Raising Low self-esteem,* 2020). That spells out disaster, especially if you are someone who is looking for a change in life and trying to find their true passion and purpose.

Now comes the part where we learn how to overcome low self-esteem and confidence. Remember the exercise I gave you earlier on? It is time for you to review the list.

The task is quite simple: identify your weaknesses and challenge them, one by one. If you feel like you cannot socialize, then start by socializing with at least one new person every day. If you feel you look old-fashioned or unattractive, go for a new hairstyle, change your glasses to something more trendy, go for a wardrobe change. The possibilities are endless, and every attempt you make will boost your self-confidence level higher.

On that list, now jot down five things you like about yourself, or that someone else finds good about you. Highlight those in your routine activities while working on your weaknesses. This may be a bit time consuming, but before you know it, people will start noticing you a lot more. You will feel that positive energy encircling you with each passing day. Eventually, you would reflect back and look at this day as the turning point, and that is where I would love to say "You're welcome!"

The Social Circle

The people in our lives, our friends, acquaintances, everyone we interact with, they all play their respective roles in our lives. The social circle was once considered as a group of people one would prefer to talk to, hang out with, all in physical presence. Now, with the invention of social media, our social circle has seemingly expanded.

While many may believe they may have over 1000 friends on Facebook, I assure you that most cannot even name 50 people they have met in real life. Most of these so-called friends are just online 'contacts' and nothing more. They may occasionally "like" our posts or publish a comment, and that is all that they can do. However, even that seems to play some effect on our life.

Each day that passes by, we do something which makes us want to publish a status update on our social media platforms, to let the world know what it was that we did. We immediately tie hopes that people will be surprised, impressed, or pass great comments. Some of them actually do, but we may end up hitting ourselves in the head for that one comment that says:

"So what?"

Similarly, when we hang out with friends, we share our achievements, catch up on gossip, and talk about all past shared experiences and memories. While doing so, someone often will touch upon a topic that somehow makes us uncomfortable. To make matters worse, we are eventually asked to participate in the conversation, and that is where things can go a bit sideways.

You are immediately met with laughter or a joke that you initially laugh at, but something inside you starts dying. This is quite a common occurrence. Our social circle decides what kind of person we can become. If the circle comprises of people who are into mischief, we would eventually follow them by getting up to some mischief of our own. If they are a group of people who maintain their physiques, we would do the same. These are both voluntary acts and involuntary ones as well. They are voluntary because we carry out these acts willingly, just because we wish to remain a part of this social circle. For exactly the same reason, these actions are involuntary as well, because we are left with no choice. If we wish to be a part of a certain group, we need to do what they are doing.

Sounds familiar, right? This is where things could have been different. I am not at all against socializing. I love to socialize and meet new people, but there is no point in bending your rules and changing yourself to become someone you are not, and into something that is taking you away from your own goals, values, and passion. It is best to avoid such social groups as much as possible.

Upon close observation, I learned that most successful people surround themselves with other successful people. You would never see billionaires being friends with addicts or people who love to cause problems or get involved in activities that are neither productive nor fruitful. They would always be with people who maintain a high profile, look after themselves, and always have a positive vibe about them. Try it yourself, and you too will need to go through the same process of changing yourself to become more like them. This is where it is perfectly okay to change your habits.

Such social circles normally follow a strict routine of exercise and healthy activities. Not only would you be adopting a better lifestyle, but you would also be making new friends and acquaintances who would actually help you in making you more successful.

Since we are talking about life-changing experiences, recall that I asked you to promise yourself a few things. One of them was honesty. Let us put that honesty to a little test.

Grab your pen and paper and write down how you feel your current social circle is. Are they negative people, or perhaps passive? Are they the kind of people who would walk away when you really need them, or vice versa?

Clear your mind and focus on all the traits of your social circle. Once you have an answer, we can move forward.

I hope you were able to come to a conclusion. If your answer is positively good, it is okay to include them in your life. If the answer is no, or if your answer has even the slightest shadow of a doubt, I would advise you to find yourself a better social circle.

If a given type of social circle changes how we are in life, there is no doubt that every one of us would like to stick around with only the finest people. Since we are talking about changing ourselves and our lives for the better, a better social circle is needed. Find the people who would elevate you to newer heights, help you in achieving success, and assist you in pursuing your dreams and passion. You know you have the right social circle once you feel they help you to be the best version of yourself. I assure you the results are well worth the search.

Past Failures

Memories; they linger on. We make memories and some are made for us. This is how the world works. Sometimes, these memories are better times while for others, they reflect a hollow and dark past.

These memories have a funny way of latching on to us. Our brain tends to experience everything but remember only a few of these memories. The question is, who decides what needs to be remembered and what needs to be forgotten? If you think it is more of a natural process, you are mistaken. In fact, it is our very own choice that provides importance to some memories and ignores others altogether. Our mind only follows our instructions and stores some while deleting others.

Our brain functions just like a computer. You select which file you wish to save, which obviously is important. At the same time, you can select which file you wish to delete, denoting that the said file is irrelevant or useless.

We attach emotional importance and significance to these memories. If you were to write down all your good memories and your bad ones as well, the bad ones would outnumber the better memories. That is because these bad memories are filled with failures, shock, traumatic experiences, or sad losses. We quickly attach significance to these events, so the mind saves them. If we could train our minds to let go of these memories, we might soon come out as a happier person.

In a similar fashion, our past failures latch on to us, and these genuinely create barriers between us and our pursuit of happiness. You may have once tried to do something and failed miserably. The guilt, the shame, and the way others laughed at you, it all adds up to become a traumatizing experience. Once that happens, you will never try to do that thing ever again. Why? Who exactly says you cannot do it ever again? What if you were just a child back then or ill-informed on the matter? Now, with age and experience, you have everything to ensure that you finally put this bad memory to rest.

A friend of mine once plugged two ends of a single wire in a socket. The result was a big spark and quite a jolt to the guy. For years, my friend would never even go near an electric socket. Even with the safest of settings, he would stay away from it. Recently I happened to meet him, and I was stunned to find out he went on to become an electrical engineer. Surprised? So was I.

I asked him how he was able to overcome his fear and he explained that he simply had no idea what he was doing. Somewhere in the late years of high school, he discovered he found electricity and the electric work behind it fascinating, and eventually took a leap of faith by carrying out his first few experiments. After learning about the basics and gathering the required knowledge, he was able to overcome his past failure and rewrite a new memory, one that went on to help him carve a better path for success.

If my friend was able to do it, so can you. If you continue to live in the past, you will never be able to explore the beauty that lies in the future. Do not let your past mistakes dictate your future. You are in control, and you can overcome every past failure. You are now more prepared to handle situations than you were when such memories were created.

You may be thinking it is to hard or this is too much effort, or even "I don't know if I want to do that." Think about it this way, you have been eating plain bread, and that's all you have eaten for years. How would you know if pizza, or sushi, for example, tastes amazing, if you don't take the step and give it a try? Why would you want to eat plain bread for the rest of your life?

Stretching Yourself Too Thin

We carry on doing so many things in life that often we end up stretching ourselves too thin doing meaningless things. How many times have you looked upon something and though:

"Interesting. I will surely learn about that once I am done doing this."

That 'once' never happens, does it? Running around all day, doing meaningless things such as watching television to catch up on news and sit through talk shows, or watching celebrities talk about their personal lives, it is all too pointless. Of course, to some, this may be their bread and butter, writing about celebrities and their personal lives, in which case it is perhaps okay until you find something even better.

By engaging our mind and body into such activities, the outcome is neither elevating us nor empowering us in any way. There is no empowerment in being the first one to finish a popular Netflix series. It is just wasting your time, hours and hours of it. Instead, one could go online, buy a great course to learn about healthier habits, or pick up a new skill like web development and learn all those codes. If you spend the same number of hours doing that instead of watching a flick on TV, the result would see you elevated and empowered. You would end up being more skillful than most of your peers. You would also allow more opportunities to flow your way. You can work a day job and do this as a side job for some extra cash. Alternatively, you can even hire other freelancers to work for you. Who knows, you may find so much success that you may even start your own venture, all thanks to a few hours you decided to spend wisely.

Always challenge yourself to do something you haven't done before. Do not delay learning new things because time is of the essence. Always continue to improve yourself, your health, your skills, and apply your newly gained knowledge appropriately.

Focusing on Short-term Goals

By now, we know how to overcome fear, correct our mistakes, make better friends, and all of the above. I am sure you would be feeling confident and you may have actually started to plan your short-term and long-term goals. However, before you do, it is vital that you know where your focus should be.

Imagine if Mark Zuckerberg had focused on earning money instead of creating the biggest social media entity in the world; Facebook would be much different today. This is exactly what most of us fail to understand.

Normally, our minds would focus more on what we have right now and decide not to focus much on what we could have in the next five or 10 years. We aim to focus a lot on these short-term goals in the hope that they would provide us with a sense of success, accomplishment, and a purpose. True, but that would be short-lived.

Make it a general rule of thumb: when you are planning, and your plan seems short-lived, they are not worth focusing on. If your long-term plan is to retire early, continue to focus on your target. Whatever happens in the middle is a secondary task. These secondary tasks certainly play an important role as without them, your primary objective may never be achieved. Focus on these, but your primary focus should always be the bigger picture, the end result.

THE BIG TAKEAWAY

To summarize, we learned:

- There are barriers that keep us from pursuing our passion and purpose.
- To find, identify, and pursue our purposes in life, we should:
- Stop fearing and conquer our fears.
- Seek out new opportunities.

- Move out of our comfort zone.
- Increase our self-confidence.
- Change our social circle.
- Be with successful people who bring out the best of us.
- Stop paying attention to the naysayers.
- Not allow past failures to dictate our future.
- Overcome and conquer our past failures.
- Avoid wasting time with meaningless activities.
- Set out long-term goals and focus on these.

All that is good takes time. Never settle for shortcuts and always move forward, knowing that you have everything it takes to make it through.

In the next chapter, we will be looking at step two, which will allow us to explore how we can find our 'drive' and how we can get going in the right direction. Quite a few interesting things lined up, and I simply cannot wait to get started.

"To live is the rarest thing in the world. Most people exist, that is all."

— OSCAR WILDE

STEP 2 - DETERMINE WHAT DRIVES YOU

For us to do anything in life, we need to have a passion. Without passion and motivation, we cannot be bothered to work or to do anything remotely productive. Despite having all the purpose in life, all the possible success right at your doorstep, you cannot do much but see it all go to waste.

Think of it this way. For any vehicle to operate, it needs to have the necessary components like the gear, the engine, the wheels, and tires, not forgetting a driver. However, despite having all that, it will still not go anywhere if it is lacking the fuel that feeds the engine and springs life into the vehicle. Much like this example, we too need that fuel, and that fuel is passion. It is this passion that drives you forward, makes you do things you may have never done before, and drives you to achieve newer heights of success.

Finding what drives you forward can be a bit tricky. More often than not, I have seen people believing that they have a passion for something because they just can't stop thinking about it. It just so happens that such actions only add to your drive, but these are not the actions or aspects where your drive or passion originates from. You would know if you are passionate about something because you would do more than just thinking; you would work to ensure whatever your passion is, continues onward.

It is important to point out that passion alone cannot get you through. To truly seek out your passion and live it, you need motivation. Both motivation and passion are interlinked. Put it this way, remove the passion and you lose your motivation. Similarly, if you take away the motivation, you will never seek out your passion. One cannot exist without the other.

For us to take the second step in our five-step guide, we must now explore and figure out what drives us to move forward. We need to find out just what makes us feel like we have got this and that we can achieve the short-term and long-term goals we have planned for ourselves. We need to learn how to avoid falling for the obvious traps and move ahead to seek out our passion with enough motivation to see us all the way through.

IN PURSUIT OF PASSION

There is no easier way to say this, so I will just get it over with. For you to find your true passion, you quite literally need to stop everything you may be engaged in and spare quite a bit of time. You will need to go into some deep thoughts and dig out that passion from within. This takes time, it might even take a few days or weeks, but once again, the results are well worth the wait.

"Oh, man! A few weeks?"

Unfortunately, there is no book or expert on earth that can help you find your true passion in an instant or in a fixed time frame. While there are many reasons why such delays occur, the most prominent reason is the people themselves. Depending on how quick they are to find out their true passion, the time would vary.

For us to proceed anywhere in life, we need to know our passion and we need to gain the right motivation to support it as well. The entire point of this book is to ensure you never stop and never look back while working towards leading a far better life. To live your life to the fullest, it is time to let the inner child speak.

Let yourself feel younger again and find out what that younger version of you was always fond of doing.

This would be an ideal time to grab that pen again and start scribbling down the ideas you think could be your passion. It does not have to be something you are good at. It can possibly be something you have always dreamed of learning or doing, but you never had the chance to do so. Whatever it may be, playing soccer, learning how to play the guitar or the piano, being a performer, being a motivational speaker, or even being a Formula One race driver, write it down.

You may have hundreds of ideas, but focus primarily on the ones to which you instantly connect and relate to. Pick out the ones that make your heart skips a beat just at the mere mention of them. Take two to five minutes at most on this activity and once done, put the notepad aside for now.

I hope you managed to put in a few ideas on that blank piece of paper. Well done! The reason I asked you to write it down is to first allow yourself to explore your own mind. I have no idea who you may be, where you may live, or what you may be doing, but I am quite certain that you know yourself better than anyone else. If anyone can help you with figuring out your passion, it is you.

Once you are done, ask your peers and colleagues what their passion is and how they were able to discover it. Some of them may have an answer, while most would just have no clue if they even have a passion. Focus on the ones who provide you with some inspiring thoughts.

Speaking out of experience, almost everyone I have met, who holds a passion for something, usually resorts to reading about it or researching about it on the internet. They may have physical copies of books on a particular subject, plus souvenirs or mementos which might link to their inner passion. Look around your own house. There is every possibility that you may come across something that genuinely interests you and makes your inner self a little bit excited. This could be in the kitchen, or your library, or in your computer, or even on your phone.

Inspirations come from everywhere; all you need is a watchful eye. The instant you spot something that motivates you to do something better, note it down somewhere. These breadcrumb trails will eventually lead you to explore your true passion and find out just what it is that you have been suppressing all this time.

Focus on the positive things which drive you forward, the things which provide you with a sense of positivity; the ones which encourage you to do better and make you more engaged are most likely connected to your real passion.

I had always loved the idea of speaking in public and helping others through my words. I was inspired by great personalities and was always mesmerized by the way they used their words to encourage entire nations. Churchill, Martin Luther King, John F. Kennedy, these were the names I would often recall before I spoke. I always wanted to speak as freely, as effectively and as powerful as they once did, and lo and behold; I found my passion at a very young age. Yes, it did kind of fade away once I was in my early 20s, but after my accident, I had the time and opportunity to dive deep into my thoughts and I came across this.

Upon recovery, I started noticing just how good I was at speaking and how it made me feel when I spoke in public. The applause, the spotlight, the ability to move the crowd with your words, it all started coming back. I had books on the shelf, filled with teachings about the art of public speaking. When I was browsing through what I wanted to pursue as a degree, the current choice immediately stood apart. I knew I had a passion for speaking and I finally embraced it.

It took me a life-altering accident to figure out my passion. It wasn't easy, but with perseverance, I made it through. The thing to remember is that you should never give up your search. You might just be a step away from discovering your true passion, and giving up at this point would only impact you negatively.

Let us further explore how we can find our passion. You can use your notepad and jot down ideas as they appear. There is a possibility that you may be able to identify a trend, or some of them may be related to each other in more ways than one. Every little bit helps, so be sure to note down each and every idea that seems to spark curiosity or excitement.

One fine way is to carve a bit of time for yourself in the morning. Ideally, you should do this before you leave for your work. Sit in a comfortable place and breathe in and out for a few minutes. While doing so, ensure to remove any excess thoughts from your mind. You will need to engage in some self-reflection exercises. It is also a good idea to switch your phone off or put it on silent mode just for a short while.

Once you are in your zone, start thinking about the day that lays right ahead of you. How do you feel about it? Are you looking forward to carrying out your duties? Are you comfortable and happy when you perform them? Take your time and think matters through. If possible, write them down on a paper after five minutes of deep thinking.

Repeat the same exercise the next day; however, change the question this time around. You can go for anything as long as it provokes your inner self and allows you to explore your own state of mind. These questions can be:

- Are you happy today? If so, what are you happy about?
- Do you feel exhausted or tired?
- Did you sleep well last night?
- Are you lacking motivation?
- Are you agitated or angry? If so, why?

The idea behind the exercise is to link these emotions and feelings to whatever it is that you are doing. Let us assume that you answered you were unable to sleep last night. Ask yourself what kept you up? Was it a movie? Was it a late night out, or was it the stress of a pending assignment at work?

If you felt angry or agitated, try and find out what action is causing you to feel that way. By establishing a connection, you would be able to identify what makes you happy and what annoys you. Once that is sorted, you can proceed to pursue or carry on doing whatever it is that makes you happy. The happier you are, the easier it will be for you to eventually stumble upon your passion: the one thing that truly makes you happy. Discover that and your life changes forever.

Another exercise is to write down all the moments of your life which held some significance. Since this is possibly a personal matter, and you may not want to share all of that information with others, I would urge you to write it on paper instead of tapping the keypad on the screen of your cell phone or typing it in a laptop.

Think about the moments which made you feel really proud. Find out what it was that you did which led to you feeling proud of yourself. List down all the personal accomplishments you can remember. These can be small achievements like winning a spelling-bee competition at school or getting a perfect score in Math. Feel free to jot down as many accomplishments as you desire. You can also list down professional accomplishments such as acing your interview for a promotion, delivering the finest presentation, tackling an extremely difficult task and resolving it, and so on.

In this list, you can also include other things that brought a real sense of satisfaction to you. These could be things like helping someone in dire need, helping the elderly cross the street, or even helping your neighbors move their furniture. The more you add to the list, the merrier the results would be.

This compiled list, combined with the one I asked you to create earlier, would allow you to take a peek into your life, and you will be able to see which of these actions genuinely made you feel better about yourself. It is a very good possibility that your true passion may just be right there before you, written in your own words.

You could have entries like:

- Web surfing
- Helping people out
- Getting to know strangers from other cultures
- Coding

Mix them all up, and your passion just might be to create platforms where people can connect with one another. Yes, Facebook does a good job, but who knows, you might have a better idea that only needs you to start working on it to flourish. It could be anything in your case. All that remains is for you to revisit this list once again over a weekend and figure out common entries or fields of interest.

As mentioned earlier, this pursuit of finding your true passion can be time-consuming. There is always the possibility of finding yourself stuck and having no idea what to do. In such situations, interview others. Surf the web for places like Medium or Quora, and ask others how they were able to find their true passion. You would be amazed and even inspired by some of the answers you would receive.

Every human being in existence and living has a story. While they all are unique in their own ways, we can relate to most of them. This means that we can always find some inspiration as well.

If you have friends and family members whom you can talk to easily, try asking them what they believe is good about you. Your objective is not to gather praises, but to find out what is common that everyone seems to notice about you. Such a quality is always a good indicator and a perfect place to start your search from.

You can also ask them to find out where they see you 10 years from now. You can expect some to say that they have no idea where you would be, in which case it is best not to feel disappointed. However, someone is bound to provide you with their honest opinion. Remember, when asking about yourself, you should always keep an open mind and be receptive. Constructive feedback can often provide you with opportunities to identify and learn from your mistakes or shortcomings.

If someone was to come up to you and say that you are

a great person and they simply adore how you are always ready to help people out, there is still room for a 'but' in the end. Instead of interrupting them, let them speak. Be keen to learn how others see you. Anyone who can identify your flaws is surely a true friend, and their feedback would be valuable to have.

Lastly, you can always ask them to see what they think of your current situation. To you, you may just be living a good life, but to them, you might be wasting hours and hours of your time doing things that would reap you no benefits. They may be quick to point out that such activities would get in the way and cause quite a lot of problems for you in the future. Do not take that as a negative note. Instead, thank them for being honest and providing you with some valuable words upon which you would work.

You may very well be wondering how all this helps you in pursuing your passion. For anyone to pursue their passion or seek it out, they must first learn to overcome some issues they may be facing. These issues, such as being engaged in unproductive activities, can greatly hinder your progress and bar you from pursuing your goals. By improving yourself as an individual and a professional, you fare a better chance at pursuing your dreams and making them into a reality.

GOING BEYOND SUPERFICIAL

There is no denying that when it comes to motivation, most of us consider money as our biggest motivator. Granted, monetary gains do provide us with a reason to work for, but that being said, they are not your biggest motivators. If you recall, we learned that our primary focus should remain on the bigger picture. What you get at the end of the month is only a short-term gain.

Money can neither be a motivator nor a passion. Saving a lot of money to start your own business, buy a property you always wanted or use said money to go on exotic vacations, they may seem like motivation, and to some extent, you may be right. However, some of these may be short-lived, while others may require quite a lot of changes. Either way, if you have a passion and a strong motivation, there is nothing that can hold you back from making that happen.

Generally, it is observed that people who often dream about amassing significant sums of money are pursuing a different kind of status or lifestyle. Certainly changing the lifestyle or being inspired by someone you met who leads such a lifestyle is quite motivating. Everyone wants in on the action, but what about passion? What do you think is the passion here? Money? Business? Ironically, none of those.

To find that, you will have to overlook the superficial and dig a little deeper, while remaining honest to yourself. Ask yourself what would having enough money change about you?

Surely, your lifestyle can change. You may think you would buy a mansion, some supercars, hire butlers and chauffeurs, and change your wardrobe to one that reflects your wealth and status. Let us assume all that happens; what then? You just spent every dollar on buying things that were good as long as you had the finances.

Take away the money and everything would come crashing down. You would not be able to pay for the expenses, let alone generate income of significant value. All of this then looks short-lived, and hence not worth your focus.

Perhaps your passion was not to change your lifestyle but to pursue something that would not only allow you to have such a life but also live it till the end. Your passion is to find that source of earning which would require you to do something you genuinely love and are good at, which creates enough income for you to spend on all these items and still be able to continue your life and pay for your expenses. Maybe, you just do not want to spend all that money and fortune on yourself. Maybe your passion is to help the poor and the needy, and you set out to fulfill that passion by doing something significant which would fetch you such large sums of money which you then donate to such people.

To fully explore your passion, it is imperative that you understand this line:

"Do not let your success define you. Define your success on your own terms!"

Ask yourself one simple question. What is success to you? Try and define it with as many details as possible. If your success revolves around money, you are probably looking at the wrong side of the picture. You do not need to be a millionaire to be successful. Look at the founder of KFC. He was successful well before he went on to become a billionaire. He defined his own success through his exceptional recipe for fried chicken that caught everyone's attention.

Find out what success means to you and how you define it. For you to lead a truly blissful life, it is important that you create your own version of success. Yes, you can use others as inspiration, but never follow blindly what others do. It is very likely that you may end up facing different results, and that would only lead to a massive disappointment in the end.

You could potentially be hoping to follow the footsteps

STEP 2 - DETERMINE WHAT DRIVES YOU | 79

of a multi-millionaire you know, and even after acquiring the luxuries and the success, you may still feel hollow. You would feel as if you are still missing something, just like Jim Carrey pointed out. All your efforts, all the blood and sweat you put into your goals stand meaningless if you do not know what the eventual goal is, where the motivation lies and what the passion behind the entire exercise is.

Today, artificial intelligence and machine learning are much in demand. Quite a lot of success stories are emerging around that area, but this does not mean that you can join the race and emerge as the next big thing. There is always a possibility that by the time you learn all about these fields, something new will come along. You will have to go through the entire learning phase all over again just to find that something even better has replaced what you just learned.

Do not follow the societal norms and they keep on changing and evolving with time. Find your passion that has remained consistent, even if that is something as simple as developing websites, or speaking in public. The biggest motivator is your success and how well you have defined it. Remind yourself daily about how great it will feel to have achieved this long-term goal. Envision your future and where you would like to see yourself 10 years from today. That would serve you as a real motivation. You already have the passion, simply work on it.

The best thing about working on your passion, or where your heart lies, is that the hardest tasks would always tickle your fancy and appear enjoyable. For anyone who puts their heart into something, every task is a new opportunity and every challenge is interesting.

Before we go on to end the chapter and move towards step three, there is one quite important thing I would like to mention. Quite a lot of people tend to believe they have discovered their true calling, and most of them are actually right. However, just because you found your passion, whether it is your personal fitness, speaking, singing, composing music, creating websites or games, do not quit your day job just yet. It will take some time for you to brush up on your skills, acquire the desired knowledge, and land an opportunity. Once that happens, feel free to say goodbye to your old job.

Sir James Dyson attempted well over 5000 times before he was able to finally hit success. This goes to show that we may not be successful in achieving our true goals and purpose immediately. All good things take time, and we just need to learn how to be patient.

You are the keeper of your story, your pros and cons, and your secrets. Explore your mind and dig out that passion from within. Find what actions lead you to feel better about yourself, increase your motivation as you go, and keep your goals in sight. Follow the routines and the healthier approach to life, find better people to guide you along the way, and you would start drawing yourself closer to the realization of your goals. The journey is not done yet, we still have quite a bit to cover before I am finally able to say:

"You now know all you need to know. Go and live your life!"

"It is better to be hated for what you are than to be loved for what you are not."

— ANDRE GIDE

STEP 3 - THINK ABOUT THE FUTURE IN LINE WITH YOUR STRENGTHS AND VALUES

This is quite an important step. The previous two were more like the tip of an iceberg. This is where things start to get a lot more serious.

We live in a world that is populated by billions of others around us. Regardless of which city, country, or even continent they hail from, everyone has a set of values, traditions, and rules they abide by. These matter quite a lot, especially if you are trying to change everything about your existence and switch on 'life' mode.

Our goals, based on our passion, are deep and meaningful to us. Such goals are always long-term. When we pursue these long-term goals, it is understood and quite obvious that they would not provide us with immediate results. This means we cannot tie false hopes that seeking such purpose and goals would fetch us a sense of gratification. They will take time and instead will provide us with a far better result than just gratification.

I do understand that we are human beings, and being human means we are bound to make a mistake or two at times. This means you may be pursuing a goal which you may think is long-term. You may achieve it sooner and feel that 'high' but what follows immediately is the realization that the 'high' just faded. This is only because you had actually set your focus on a short-term goal.

Using your own unique set of skills, passion, talent, and capabilities, set your mind to your own long-term goals. Remind yourself that all the joys in between are just short-lived and that you must soldier on until you have achieved and realized your ultimate goal. By the time you reach there, you would have already spent a significant number of years happily. The goal itself would just be the icing on the cake, and you would have all the time in the world to savor it as much as you please.

Our third step, then, brings us to a point where we must forget the past, put a hold on our present and start looking at our future. The third step takes us deeper into ourselves, to discover, learn, and identify our core values. It is with these values and strengths that we can think and plan for a probable future. Anything that seems odd, wrong, weird, or even uncomfortable will automatically be discarded at this point.

SETTING THE RIGHT GOALS

Suppose a friend of yours wishes to be a supermodel. She has a passion for fashion, she practically lives and breathes cosmetics, is masterful at exquisite wardrobe selection, and knows everything about luxury perfumes. She certainly has everything she needs, but when asked about her values, she says this:

"I am not comfortable posing before the camera"

The problem here is quite clear. By being unable to pose for the camera, there is no way even the trendiest of ladies can have a shot at becoming a model. Why do you think that is?

In such a case, there could be a few logical explanations.

1. She has suffered from some traumatizing experience in the past with cameras.
2. She may have been led to believe that all models need to acquire indecent poses.
3. Her values and norms do not allow her to pose for the camera.

All three could be possible, but notice how the last one seems to make more sense? If that is the case, perhaps modeling isn't her cup of tea. She can still seek out her passion and do something incredible in the field of fashion. She could become a designer and design fashionable clothes, or she could join a firm and be a part of a fashion-conscious team like Ralph Lauren. Not only would she be sticking to her values, but she would at the same time be seeking her passion.

Setting goals can often be complicated. There is so much on offer, and every day something completely new and unique keeps on emerging. The possibilities are endless, but not all possible opportunities are worth going after.

This is where you need to dive back into your mind and find out more about what your values and strengths are. The good news is that you have already noticed some of your strengths thanks to the exercises in the previous chapter. Remember the list I asked you to make? Have a look at it again. This time, focus only on what your strengths are, or what others believe your strengths can be. Circle them out and write them down on a separate piece of paper. We will be reviewing that later as well.

The goals you will go on to set cannot be as small as "being helpful" or "to be a better person" as these can be achieved with minimum efforts. Besides, from what we have learned previously, and what we will learn ahead, will automatically push us to bring our better versions out and let go of the type of person we are right now. These goals have to be meaningful and significant enough in nature. If your long-term goal is to become a successful entrepreneur or to establish a business with multiple outlets, you are definitely onto something bigger and more meaningful. This means you will have to constantly push yourself forward, always seeking out motivation and following your dreams with passion to achieve this mammoth task. Surely, you cannot invest a million dollars today and expect profits to automatically flow in the next day.

Such larger goals will give meaning to your life. You may even have to change quite a lot of things about yourself in order to ensure you live up to your own expectations and carry on with your pursuit. At the very same time, you need to ensure that these goals are both personalized and achievable. Do not go on setting goals that are either impossible to achieve or are just plain daft in nature. To help you set such goals, you will need to fully understand your strengths, your weaknesses, and your values.

Everybody follows a set of rules and holds certain values. These could be religious, ethnic, or something that runs in the family. There are those who love to drink, and then there are those who hate the idea of alcohol in their drinks. There are those who value looks and then there are those who value the nature of a person. Everyone has a personal preference.

These essential values may not bother you much at this point, but let us for a second assume that you are someone who values morals and ethics. Imagine that you are presented with an opportunity that pays you really well, but the work requires you to do things that you believe are neither morally nor ethically correct; what would you do?

If you hold values diametrically opposed to the work on offer, you would simply pass on the job or business opportunity, and seek better opportunities instead. Even if you would have been being paid handsomely, if deep down something did not feel right and there was a clear contradiction with your own set of values, you will always part ways or pass the opportunity.

In another setting, imagine working in an environment where there are plenty of growth opportunities in terms of rank and financial gains. The only thing you would need to do is to be in your boss's good books, and you are good to go. While initially it may sound good enough for you, upon joining you realize that those who work really hard and well are often overlooked, while those who continue to please their bosses with other favors keep on growing. It would not take much longer before you either have a word with your seniors or simply hand in your resignation.

Values play a very important role in life. When setting out your future goals, it is vital that you keep true to your values and seek out goals where such values are highlighted. If you aim to set goals that go against your values, you will never be able to fully lead a happy life, because every day you would wake up knowing that you are letting yourself down. That is not what we are here to do.

To help you further understand, let us look at something called the Maslow's hierarchy. If you are a business student, you may already be familiar with this.

Maslow designed a pyramid that reflects a hierarchy. This hierarchy, however, is quite a unique one. The triangle is divided into five segments, from bottom to top. These five segments are:

- Physiological needs (food, water, warmth, rest)
- Safety needs (security, safety)
- Belongings and love needs (intimate relationships, friends)
- Esteem needs (prestige and feeling of accomplishment)

- Self-actualization (achieving one's full
  potential)

The first two are classified as basic needs. Obviously, everyone needs these and without them, we are bound to perish. The next two, belongings and love needs, and esteem needs, are classified as psychological needs. These are the things which provide us psychological satisfaction. The final phase is classified as self-fulfillment needs. This is the one we are trying to reach.

As the pyramid starts from the bottom, things are simple, but as it goes up, things, just as the pyramid, start narrowing down and become harder to acquire. It is very rare to see people achieve their maximum potential. Only one percent of the world population has managed to achieve this. That said, that one percent is still quite a lot of people who actually end up achieving complete self-actualization.

Self-actualization is the phase where one truly achieves everything they had envisioned and planned in life. No wonder why only one percent of people actually managed to do that. You might be surprised that this one percent might not include some of the most famous names you may have thought of. It is very much possible that despite being so popular and successful, they may be missing out on meaningful relationships, or they may even be worrying about their safety needs. It happens, and we have all seen and heard such stories before, haven't we?

When setting goals, businessmen and corporations use this hierarchy for marketing. People who pursue self-improvement also resort to using it to figure out where they stand and what they would need to do in order to achieve a higher rank.

Suppose you are someone who is struggling to find a meaningful relationship, you are obviously in the second classification. After getting into said relationship, you would be able to tick the box off and move on to achieve other needs and eventually move up the rank to pursue higher goals.

In most cases, we are already able to fulfill our basic needs. Setting up goals that revolve around them is both pointless and a waste of effort. Look beyond your basic needs or any needs which are already being fulfilled. As long as you have a roof over your head and your meals for the day, both your basic and safety needs are covered.

Now, keeping your core values and strengths in view, use this pyramid and target the top rank of self-actualization. Fill out the missing bits and see what you already have and what you need to obtain. Pretty soon, you should be able to work out a path that leads you to your self-actualization.

You may have basic needs covered, you may also have the safety needs provided for: seek out what else you have and where it fits. Find out what is missing and where does that go? One after the other, fill out the spaces and after a few attempts, you should know what you need to do along the way to fully live your life to the maximum.

Using the above pyramid, you can come up with significant and meaningful goals, and perhaps even fill out those gaps. To get you started, here are some popular ideas:

- Pursuing creative abilities
- Mastering scientific expertise
- Starting your own business
- Patenting a product
- Helping out others
- Spreading love
- Volunteering for community work
- Starting your own charity
- Becoming a mentor to someone

The choices are endless. You can set achievable goals and try to aim for those. When setting goals, it is always good to set both short-term and long-term goals. The short-term goals will help you with your motivation and provide you with a sense of achievement. These short-term goals are practically the best way to provide yourself with a purpose and lead a life fulfilling that purpose.

This brings me to another very important aspect. When you sit down planning your goals, there are a few things that may often pop up, and they may even sound like a solid plan. However, not all that you think up is worth chasing.

Sometimes, it is often easy to get mixed up between what we want and what we need. It is somewhat surprising that many still do not understand the difference between wants and needs. These are two terms that mean and imply completely different things.

The word 'want' is associated with something we either wish to acquire or possess. On the other hand, the word 'need' refers to anything that is vital or essential for us to live. So, one may think they wish to buy or rent a house or an apartment, in reality, however, it is their need to have shelter or a place they can call home. See how easy we can confuse ourselves?

Similarly, when setting goals by following Maslow's hierarchy, it is quite easy for us to stumble across some desires and some needs. Ensure that you know the difference between the two and assign them to the relating classification.

You may be fancying a new car, but if you really think about it, all you need is a means of transportation, something that you can rely upon to take you from point 'A' to point 'B' and that is it. Whether you aim to buy a Tesla or a 10-year-old Toyota, they will still get the job done in a similar fashion.

There is no denying that these wants at times can be too tempting. One such case is traveling. Everyone loves to do so, and you cannot ignore the fact that it is indeed a good way to explore the world. However, even such travels fall under the definition of desires. It is a luxury that many cannot afford, but at the same time, it is only a short-lived joy that ends as soon as you return to your normal routine activities.

Traveling may enlighten you with knowledge, but vacations still do not provide you with a purpose to seek in life. Some may argue that through travels, you get to learn a lot and get to know the world better than what is being portrayed on the media. Yes, that is quite right. However, read that line once again and you will immediately know that the purpose of travel is not to explore the world, it was always to learn.

Try not to let your needs and wants get tangled up. Explore your thoughts clearly and know what affects you in the long-term. Things that you cannot live without, such as food, water, and shelter, are always categorized as needs. The rest is usually a desire which would certainly add to your life but would not change your life if not achieved.

Speaking of travels, our goals, especially the longer-term ones, also require a bit of critical thinking and clear planning. It is not only important but mandatory for you to know how you plan on executing said plan and make things work for you. The goal, so far, is just an idea scribbled on a piece of paper. Your current situation is your point 'A' and your goal is the destination, or in this case point 'B'. If you do not have any idea how you will go from 'A' to 'B' you can never really proceed nor gauge your success. You know where you want to go, but unless you have a route planned out, you will not be going anywhere.

It is said that one should hope for the best but prepare for the worst. I do not mean to alarm you but there is every chance that even simple goals would present you with challenges, roadblocks, and other issues. As an effective planner, plan well ahead of time. Think matters through and think of all the possible issues you may face along the way. Even the tiniest ones matter here because you would prepare yourself for every kind of situation, and that will always serve you with an added advantage.

When you eventually stumble into issues, your plan will come to your rescue and you will always know what needs to be done because you were already expecting it to happen. Think of issues that you can face and how you will face them. In simpler words, devise your strategy correctly, and you should find it relatively easy to deal with these issues head-on instead of retreating from them.

All this positivity and drive can often make you feel a little overconfident. When that happens, we tend to put our guard down and are immediately bombarded by problems from all directions. Never let your guard down and never let your mind be fooled into thinking you are invincible. The more prepared you are, the better you can tackle these issues as they come.

EXPECTATIONS VS REALITY

The biggest challenge in life that we all face at some point in time is knowing what to expect in the future. Sure, we can set expectations and hope the results would be as we want them to be when we get there. The reality, however, is always a little different. It can be better than what we expected or it can end up on the opposite side of the spectrum. Cracking that is one of the toughest things anyone can do.

No book or guide can provide you with a clear direction, nor predict the exact result. There are always variations in every case.

Take a simple cooking recipe as an example. If I was to whip up some chicken soup, mine would taste a little different as compared to the one you may make. We both would have the same recipe but the difference would always exist.

Following the same example, if we were to set goals in life, the reality at the end would always differ for each of us. Some of us may end up acquiring a lot more while others may end up disappointed. Why do you think that happens?

When setting goals, we often end up with goals that may sound good but are too unrealistic to happen in our lifetime. Since we are talking about long-term goals, anything can happen in the middle of our journey to self-realization. All those tiny events and decisions can greatly alter the course and leave us with a different version of the goal that was neither expected nor intended.

To ensure that we do not end up doing that, it is a fine

practice to set realistic goals. While I have mentioned it before, I felt it would serve as a reminder to us all to revisit our ideas and ensure that they are both personalized and achievable. You cannot wake up one day and decide to launch a business as good as Amazon and expect it to happen easily. There is a possibility that you may have no idea about all the work that goes on behind the scenes which makes Amazon work as it does. If that is the case, you will first need to alter your life, learn about those technicalities and then start a business, and that, at least at this point, is hard if not impossible.

There is no harm in trying. I always encourage everyone to explore their passion and expertise, but I also remind them to keep things simple and realistic. It is through this realistic approach that you will find growth. By setting unrealistic expectations, you will never gain fruitful results and end up disappointing yourself. The result would see you clueless and frankly worried.

One fine way to manage your goals is to break it down into segments. These should be achievable milestones that you can continue to work upon. It is just like taking a 100-mile drive. After every 10 miles, you know you have covered a certain part of the distance and how much more to expect.

If you intend to pursue starting a business, break the idea down into segments. Think of all the things you will need to do such as registering your business, setting up an office, arranging the legal papers, acquiring clients, marketing, sales, income or revenue generation, and eventually expansion. Through this, you can focus on each one of these individually, one at a time. By doing so, you are more likely to succeed, enjoy the success of each milestone, and feel more motivated than ever before. There is no denying the fact that success highly fuels our motivation. Whatever we aim to do, we do it to taste success, to feel accomplished, and to know we were able to do something we planned on doing. By breaking the goal into these little milestones, you are bound to make things more simple and realistic. With each milestone you pass, you will be more motivated to pursue the next step, and the chain will go on until you eventually hit the jackpot.

At this point, you may have set quite a few goals, and you might have even managed to break them down, and that is good. The next important thing is to know how to prioritize them.

Surely, you cannot expect to go out chasing all your dreams and goals at the same time. Some goals may take priority over others. Some of these may be essential, especially the ones which are time-constrained.

STEP 3 - THINK ABOUT THE FUTURE IN LINE WITH Y... | 101

Those which do not alter or change with time can perhaps be delayed or given a lower priority.

Have another look at the goals you have set. Start by writing a letter 'T' next to the ones which are time-constrained. Next, write 'U' to mark the ones which are urgent and must be done within a certain time frame. Once again, remember that you should only keep goals that are achievable and realistic.

After these markings, you should now have goals that are urgent, time-constrained or both. Automatically, your first priority would go to the ones which are marked as both time-constrained and urgent in nature. Follow those with the ones which are marked as urgent and finally the ones which are time-constrained. You can modify the list as per your requirements, but the basic idea is to ensure you know which goals take priority and need to be catered first.

On some occasions, you may have to tackle two different goals at the same time. In such cases, you will need to ensure you plan well ahead and find out how exactly you would be handling these. Once again, remember to take notes of any possible issue you may face when handling two or more goals at the same time. This would allow you to prepare yourself and be in a better position to handle issues when they eventually present themselves.

Like everything, these goals also have a starting time and an estimated deadline. Our long-term goals would remain long-term unless you decide when you want to start working on them. Do not let excitement get the better of your judgment. You may not be prepared to begin a life-altering journey immediately.

Think about your current situation and how you can make time for these goals. Work out a workable plan and then decide when is the right time to commence your work. You should be able to manage enough time to dedicate yourself and your efforts to achieving your goals. Until such time, it is best to hold back on your starting date, unless your immediate goals do not require you to put in a lot of effort.

Goals can take a while to achieve. They certainly demand a lot of attention and consistency. There is no point in seeking out goals if you are not too sure whether you would be able to continue pursuing them after a few years. As human beings, we have a nasty tendency of deviating from our set targets. Try and keep yourself occupied and do not feel let down if you are not immediately achieving the success you thought you would. Give it the time it needs and carry on with your plan.

This brings us to the end of this chapter. By now, you should have something solid right before you; your own defined goals and how you plan on achieving them. Yes, it will take a bit of trial and error at first, but once you start, there will be no turning back. Keep your motivation high and remain consistent. You will encounter issues along the way, but as long as you prepare in advance, you should not find it difficult to manage them. Keep these goals somewhere where you can review them every now and then. As a self-motivation exercise, strike off the milestones as you achieve them. Your target is not to strike these off quickly, but to ensure they are fully dealt with and realized. We are seeking a quality life, one that feels fulfilled and makes us feel happy. Speed or quantity is not what we seek.

In the next chapter, we will be starting our fourth step. The chapter will take you through some of the daily actions you can, should, and at times must take to further help you lead a better life. You already know how to set goals, how to utilize your passion and make the most of your given situation. It is time to see what else can be done to further amp up the experience.

"There are only two ways to live your life. One is as though nothing is a miracle. The other is as though everything is a miracle."

— ALBERT EINSTEIN

STEP 4 - TAKE DAILY ACTION

Setting up goals is perhaps a difficult task. It is time-consuming as we learned earlier, and already you may have made some modifications or altered a few things. As I mentioned earlier, things change with time, and so do priorities. The beauty of setting long-term goals is that they rarely change unless you have genuinely stumbled across the opportunity of a lifetime. But even then, your goals need action, and without action, they are nothing more than mere words written somewhere in a diary or a notebook.

The fourth step of this program aims to highlight the importance of taking a few important steps and making them into a habit so that they are carried out on a regular and daily basis. Through these steps, you will achieve things a little easier and they would add value to your life and purpose.

Actions of any kind, big or small, create a difference. Our goals in life are highly dependent on the actions we take. These actions, depending on what they are, can either take you closer to your goals or pull you in the opposite direction. With that said, there still are people who plan the best plans, lay down a perfect strategy on how to achieve said plan, have everything that would virtually guarantee success, and still, they do not take the necessary actions.

Everyone is busy either wasting their time thinking about what could be, or they are carrying out significant actions without realizing a sense or a purpose. In either case, people end up missing the point, and it all ends up in disappointment. My job is to share all the necessary information to ensure that it does not happen with you.

KNOW HOW TO TAKE ACTION

One of the biggest misconceptions we have is that we will truly be able to live our purpose after acquiring and achieving a number of larger milestones and that anything before it cannot be classified as purpose. As it turns out, it is quite the contrary.

All the actions we take in our daily lives contribute to life itself and reflect our purpose in one way or another. Driven by our passion, these actions either allow us to do something truly amazing or end up doing something we later regret in life. Finding your purpose is all about those small, mindful, and premeditated everyday decisions you take. These seemingly insignificant actions are what collectively add to our purpose and in the end, provide us with a sense of achievement.

In the previous chapter, we came across Maslow's hierarchy. The entire pyramid structure follows the same principle. While everyone is trying to achieve that ultimate goal, our daily actions, significant or otherwise, contribute to the bigger picture.

To pursue your passion and purpose, and to ensure that you remain consistent, start by doing one small and relative action every day. This could be anything depending on your passion. If you wish to be a motivational speaker like me, start with simple actions like self-reflecting on your thoughts, or trying to build up your charisma by standing in front of a mirror and talking.

These actions may seem small, but I assure you that you would be thanking yourself when you eventually achieve your goals. Without these petty actions, all of your goals would have limited themselves to that piece of paper you wrote them on.

These actions do not need to be big at all. Start small with manageable actions. They do not have to be life-defining either. As long as you continue to carry these actions out once or twice a day, they will soon become a part of your habits and routine. Once that happens, you will feel yourself evolve and grow accordingly.

Let us assume you wish to become a commercial pilot. You will need to go through hundreds of flying hours before you are even allowed to fly a small plane on your own. Why? Simply because you have much to learn and it takes quite a bit of time for you to adopt certain actions as a part of your routine. Once that happens, only then are you fully capable of taking off, cruising at higher altitudes, and eventually landing the aircraft safely.

Let those physical and psychological changes settle into your mind as a vital part of your life. They will continue to provide you with a purpose and a meaning. If you choose to help one soul every day, it may simply seem insignificant. Surely, helping a single soul would not change anything, but have you ever thought just how many souls you would have helped after a month, a year, or after a decade if you continue doing this every day? That is a massive number, and the thought of doing so alone puts our hearts at ease.

Make these actions become positive habits for you to follow every day. Not only would they start to create an impact on your mind, but they would also create some impact on those around you. Here are some great examples for you to draw inspiration from. use these as a guideline only. You can further add or modify the list as per your own situation.

LEARN TO SET SMART GOALS

Unless you are a business student, you may have noticed that I mentioned the word 'smart' in all caps. That was not a typing error. For those who are not aware, SMART is an abbreviation for goals which are:

- **Specific** - Simple, sensible, significant
- **Measurable** - Meaningful, motivating
- **Achievable** - Attainable
- **Relevant** - Reasonable, realistic, resourced and result-based
- **Time-bound** - Time-based or time-limited

Large and successful organizations, corporations, industries, and even individuals follow this method.

Obviously, there are some technicalities involved to fully utilize this method and be able to create SMART goals. Let us look at each of the elements here in a little more detail and find out just how we can create better goals using this method.

Specific

Your goal should always be very specific and clear. It should contain no ambiguity or confusion. This is important as clear goals allow us to focus on the task and find the motivation we need. Otherwise, we would be running around in circles, trying to figure out what we are supposed to do.

When drafting your goals, a good way to begin is by asking yourself a few important questions. These are the famous five 'W' questions, and they are:

- **What** do you wish to accomplish?
- **Why** is this goal so important?
- **Who** is involved in this goal?
- **Where** is this goal located?
- By **when** do you foresee achieving this goal?

Here is a typical comparison of goals. One offers a vague concept while the other is a SMART goal, defining the specifics clearly.

1. I wish to save a lot of money - Vague, abrupt, and provides no specifications.
2. I wish to save around $10,000 in the next 12 months by continuing to work hard at the office so that I can invest the money into a startup business.

Sure enough, the second one provides you with clearer specifics. These tiny little additions provide you with a clearer picture, hence allowing you to set goals that are specific and achievable through careful planning.

Measurable

Why do you think it is important to have goals which can be measured in one way or another? Exactly! Unless you have goals that are measurable, you will never really know where you may be and how far off you are from achieving your goal. There will be no way to gauge your success or failure for the said goal. It is also possible that without measuring your goal's success, you might continue to pursue said goals even if they had been long accomplished.

A good measurable goal should be able to answer a few important questions, namely:

1. How much?

2. How many?
3. How exactly will I know when my goal is
   accomplished?

If your goal cannot provide you with these answers,
you may have to revisit your goals and find out what
part of the goal is either missing or wrong.

Achievable

Certainly, there is no point in setting out goals that are
either impossible or simply unachievable. Your goals, as
before, must be realistic, relatable, and above all achievable to be successful. Yes, it is good to set goals that
stretch your abilities, but that does not mean that even
after all the hard work, you end up with nothing. As
long as your goals can be achieved after maximum
efforts, you are good to go.

Achievable goals usually provide you with answers to
questions like:

- How can you accomplish your goal?
- How realistic is your goal, keeping your
  finances and other resources in view?

Relevant

Now this one is a little different than the rest. First of all, what exactly is a relevant goal? Aren't all goals relevant to us? As it turns out, no. If you pay good attention to the things you have learned so far, there is a chance you might strike off a few goals to further bring your list down to the ones that truly matter. These goals would be relevant not only for you but for those who are involved in this as an integral part.

As an organization, setting goals can be challenging. They go through hundreds of ideas before coming down to one that is achievable, realistic, specific, and more importantly, relevant to everyone working within the organization.

Your typical relevant goal should allow you to retain control while acquiring all the help you can get from those involved in it. A typical relevant goal would be able to provide you with answers to questions like:

- Does the goal seem worthwhile?
- Is this the perfect time for this goal?
- Does the goal match with any other efforts or needs?
- Am I the perfect candidate to reach and acquire this goal?
- Is it currently applicable in the given socio-economic environment?

If your goal is able to provide you with clear answers, carry on with your plans, and execute the goal as per desire.

Time-bound

Here is the part where you must decide whether your goal is time-bound or not. It is much like the previous exercise we carried out where I asked you to mark your goals with certain letters. However, unlike before, SMART goals are ones where you set out deadlines for your goals. Every goal you present yourself with must have a start and an end. This allows you to know just how much time you have to ensure your goals are achieved successfully. This also helps in planning your goals more smartly, to ensure you always have the upper hand.

A time-bound goal should be able to provide you with answers to questions like:

- When?
- What can be done in the next six months?
- What can be done in the next 12 months?
- What can be done today?

Now that you have learned about the SMART goal method, use that to your advantage and carry out meaningful actions that continue to contribute to your long-term goals.

You may have also noticed, or at least read somewhere on the internet, that successful people like CEOs and heads of state dedicate significant time to reading. There was once a time I didn't really understand why everyone was so fond of reading books. I wanted to know what kind of books they were reading that kept them so occupied. While there is no specific niche that they follow, they continue to read only with the intention of acquiring knowledge that is new and different. Their constant reading habits allow them to grow themselves into more successful beings because they are equipped with knowledge most of us can only dream of. However, that simply does not mean that we cannot be like them.

Add reading to your list of "things to do daily" as reading will allow you to learn a lot. This, of course, does not mean that you go on reading virtually anything you can get your hands on. Your reading material must be aligned with your core values and/or passion. If you wish to become a successful entrepreneur, read books about psychology, business, smart and innovative ideas to seek, motivational books, and biographies of success stories.

Alternatively, you can also pick up new skills that you

can enjoy acquiring and learning every day. You can pick up skills that either allow you to expand your horizons, such as photography or graphic designing, or you can go for something that keeps you calm and composed, like crocheting. Any skill you pick up along the way will go on to serve you well.

Our aim is to lead a life that feels fulfilled every single day. This means you will need to do things to maintain your life's other aspects apart from your work. These daily activities and actions can do miracles for you to keep your social life healthy, to promote your better self, to improve your relationships, and to maintain your composure. You will need to take care of all these elements to ensure a balanced life that continues to impress you and make you feel alive and living, even when you are not behind the desk at your workplace.

It also greatly helps if you speak to someone who inspires you greatly. This does not necessarily have to be a celebrity or a politician in particular. There are times you can find such inspirations right next to you. It could be a person you see every day when walking to work. It could be your spouse, who seems to know what they are doing. It could be a teacher at a school who miraculously recovered from injuries and leads as a role model for others, or you can even speak to your colleagues and co-workers.

Speaking with the inspirational characters in your life will allow you to develop a better understanding of life and how things are handled in a given situation. With technology on our side, we can make use of social media to connect with such personalities far easier than we could back in the day.

There will be times where you are met with challenges. By practicing how to remain calm and composed every day, you will be able to focus on any problem one at a time and resolve it before moving on to the next one. Trying to tackle all issues at once will only lead you to feel pressured, and the results could be anything but positive. Try not to fall for the obvious trap and handle these issues one at a time.

There are numerous actions you can think of to carry out on a regular basis. These may seem a bit inconvenient at first, maybe a touch embarrassing too, but once you start doing the same thing over and over again, you will gain the confidence to go out there and get the job done. Not only would you arrive home feeling relaxed and good about yourself, but you may have also made someone else's day by helping them out.

TO-DO LISTS - THEY ARE IMPORTANT

I mentioned quite a few of these actions and provided you with some good methods to get you going. Even after you have gone through the entire list all over again, it is a possibility that you may still end up forgetting something. Someday, you may be focusing on your task when all of a sudden you are asked to do something else. That is where you think "No worries, I know what I need to do!" You start recalling all the things you learned here and immediately, you feel like you forgot something.

"Oh, come on! Not now!"

This happens more often than I can tell. This happens to me at times as well. This is why I started to keep a to-do list, which I update every hour or so. This to-do list of mine not only reminds me of what I need to do, but it allows me to plan ahead and decide what needs to be done when.

To-do lists have been in existence for a very, very long time. Back when pharaohs were ruling their kingdoms, back when the Mughal empire dominated Asia, back when some of the most ancient civilizations existed, people would write down lists of things they wanted to achieve. They served them as reminders of what needs to be done, when, and where. Centuries later, we continue to have these around, and despite the massive changes in technology and life in general, they still provide us with the same results.

Not only is it a good idea to have a to-do list with you, but it is also seen as a professional habit and a good ethical habit in many countries. It shows just how dedicated you are to your life and work. It reflects your seriousness and willingness to achieve your targets. If something goes into that list, everyone knows it is important.

The ideal way to start with your to-do list is to write down all your tasks and ideas the night before. When your day starts, you already know what needs to be done, and you can plan accordingly and manage your activities in a way to ensure that you strike off most of these tasks.

One crucial thing to remember about your to-do list is that the goal is never to strike off all the items. In fact, the goal is to strike off only the most important ones. These are tasks like paying your bills on time, dropping your kid off at school, attending a meeting, speaking to your co-workers about an ongoing project, shopping for groceries, and such other relatable tasks. Things like calling your friend, having a drink, buying a DVD, or even stopping by a shop just to stare at a few things, it is perfectly okay to let them go unchecked.

This would only happen at the start. Once you grow habitual of maintaining your to-do list, you will soon see the pattern yourself and ultimately, you would stop including irrelevant or not-so-important tasks in your list. This would show that you, as a person, have grown more organized and know exactly how to spend your time maximizing your potential and efforts in a productive and meaningful manner.

It takes time, and a bit of practice, for anyone to master the art of making and maintaining a to-do list. However, keep practicing because the benefits of doing so are far greater than my words can describe.

By keeping a to-do list in your daily activities, you would:

- Be able to reflect upon your day and gauge how good or otherwise it was.
- Be able to identify what is important and what isn't.
- Be able to find out what kind of issues you faced when you carried out such tasks.
- Be able to feel accomplished and proud of all that you have done in the day.
- Be able to sleep comfortably, knowing you did your best.

With that said, we have now come to the end of the fourth step. It is time to move forward to our final chapter and step. In the next chapter, we will discuss one final aspect that can greatly reduce your chances of success and can often lead you to disappointment. We will learn how to avoid that before we approach the finale and set off to pursue a better life.

"I don't stop, and I won't stop until I acquire what is rightfully mine; life!"

— *ALEC MOONEE*

STEP 5 - STOP COMPARING YOUR ACCOMPLISHMENTS

It is only natural for us to seek out what others have accomplished so far in their lives. To us, it gives us an idea of how far ahead we may be or how far behind we are lagging. What many fail to understand is that there is no point in comparing yourself to others at all.

Since we are speaking about personal growth, we are only focusing on ourselves as individuals, not as a company or an organization. Businesses can and should compare themselves with their respective competitors. That is how a business would find out where they may be wrong or in what specific field do they excel or fail. Using this information, every business can work to improve their standings in the market and come out more successful. However, the same does not apply to individuals, and that is exactly what this chapter will be looking into.

The final step in our five-step guide takes us through one of the most common mistakes we end up making. The results are always far less meaningful than we might perceive. We will be looking into what makes us want to compare, who we compare ourselves to, and why is all of this meaningless. We will also be learning ways to avoid falling for such misleading actions which can clearly have an impact on us and those around us.

COMPARISON - WHY?

For all the readers, regardless of their age, geographical location, gender, and background, the most important lesson to learn is rather simple. Your goals are yours alone. They are personal and they are yours to keep, accomplish, or ignore. In other words, they are your assets.

Now, correct me if I am wrong, but would anyone allow others to comment over something they do not own? Would anyone allow others to invade their assets or properties? No. Absolutely not.

The irony is, everyone else has the same answer, but when it comes to real life, they just cannot help but pass on comments on how this goal of yours is going to fail you. They are quick to point out how someone they knew tried the same and ended up with nothing more than disappointment and embarrassment. Remind me, why exactly do we care what others say about our private matters? It is not only a sad fact of life, but it is one that often makes a completely calm and composed person lose their temper. The second you lose yours, they will continue by saying, "See? I told you!"

This happens because some people genuinely believe you will outshine and outsmart them, while others are simply jealous to see you succeed so easily. They do not care about the fact that you might be spending all your time and putting in all your energy and efforts in ensuring your goals are achieved. All they see is "how easily" you made it so far.

This is a sad truth of life. They start comparing you with others who either accomplished far too much or ended up with bitter defeat. Another simple fact, which they magically seem to ignore, is that we all have our unique strengths and weaknesses.

We all live our own lives. Not a single soul on earth can claim that they have lived exactly the same life, with the same problems, and the same strengths and weaknesses. Therefore, the entire exercise of comparing you to someone else is pointless.

On the other hand, when people seem to be minding their own business, we at times take it upon ourselves to compare how we fare against someone else. Once again, that is a mistake we end up making. The same rule that applies to society at large equally applies to you as well.

Your way of living, your current situation, your past and your possible future are yours to live. You cannot compare yourself to Bill Gates or Mark Zuckerberg. In fact, you cannot even compare yourself with someone who has miserably failed in life. Their lives and their choices are as unique as are yours.

The question that this brings us to is this - why do we still continue to compare each other despite knowing it does not matter at all? The reason lies in the way we have been brought up in our society.

Throughout the world, it is only natural for us to compare our situation with someone else's. The reality is that we are designed and programmed to function this way. We keep finding relatable aspects we can then compare ourselves with, and in the process either feel better or worse. Comparing also leads to all sorts of problems. You may compare yourself with someone you know who has yet to even discover the meaning and purpose of life, and you might think "Well, at least I am better than them" and that too is wrong. If this sentiment or thought is forwarded to the other party, surely they will feel demotivated, ridiculed, and upset. Our job is to ensure we lead a happy and fulfilling life, and a major part of that revolves around the people we interact with. If you start belittling anyone just because you think they have no clue about what they are doing, or because they are not as successful as you, you are proving yourself to be no different than the type of people whom society hates.

Comparison generally arises because of multiple reasons. These include:

- Peer pressure
- Societal expectations
- Family issues
- Professional expectations

Once you start comparing yourself with others, you will be consumed by it. It is an evil that is hard to get rid of, and it will easily derail you from your own set of rules, values, and purpose in life. All the hard work you put in will go in vain, and you will have to start all over again from scratch.

It is only natural that our minds feel both love and resentment from and towards others. While the former is perfectly okay, the latter needs attention. We need to know how we can work on our resentments and how we can do something else that is more productive and meaningful instead. Such strong and negative emotions can often cloud your judgment, leading you to believe you are doing something good, whereas you might end up doing more harm.

To resolve the issue for good, you will need to put in some effort. As always, it will take time. Remember, without your dedication, consistency and perseverance, it is not possible for you to resolve anything.

You can begin by stopping yourself from tracing anyone's accomplishment. These could be celebrities or people you know. You could be using Facebook or LinkedIn to keep track of these professionals and how they are doing in life. Stop such activities right away. Not only peeking into someone else's life is wrong, but it is also counter-productive. You are essentially wasting your time, and time is something we cannot afford to lose at all.

Once you stop keeping track of these personalities, you will eventually be free from the need to compare yourself with them ever again. Yes, you may be tempted to have a quick peek because "there's no harm in a quick peek" but do not allow yourself to give in to temptation and go back to your old habits. It takes quite a bit of courage and dedication to step out of these habits, falling back into them is perhaps the easiest thing to do.

Start changing yourself and your mindset. Start from scarcity and make your way up to abundance. Build your character, build your professional reputation, work on making a difference in your society, and try and become an example for others to draw inspiration from.

There is a quote that I have always loved from the start, and that perfectly shows why you shouldn't compare yourself with others or allow others to compare you with someone else.

"Things aren't always what they seem to be!"

I am sure you have come across this quote quite a few times. It perfectly describes the reality that we often fail to see. You may be a huge fan of Mathew Perry, Chandler from the famous tv show *Friends*. You may think he might be leading a perfect life after acquiring such fame. You would be wrong, very wrong.

Celebrities train themselves every day to look positive to the world, to reflect confidence, and to act as if everything is okay for them. Deep down, they can also suffer from horrendous issues, career-ending addictions, and life-threatening diseases, and most of us are simply unaware of those. This happens because we are so caught up with a perceived image of perfection that we see on the big screen. To us, that smile and winning attitude define everything. It is nothing more than a mask to hide the true life they lead off the screens.

Everyone on earth has issues, problems that they would never want to have in the first place. Since that is the case, the entire point of comparing ourselves to others is just foolish. Things do not come easy for all of us. Some of us have a bit of luck while others have to create their own luck; that is how life is.

Everything in life is explainable, as long as one is ready to listen intently and observe carefully. If you are among those who claim that it's not fair that you suffer more compared to your friends, try to understand that you, or anyone else for that matter, is not the judge of what in life is defined as fair and what isn't. This is quite a hard pill to swallow, but once you do that, things will make a lot more sense.

You are reading this book to define your own future and create your own success, one that you can be proud of. Your own success, however big or small it may be, has nothing to do with anyone else or their actions.

Some of us often feel that they have struck a new low point in their lives. They often feel this way because life is not turning out to be as they thought it would. Things were still okay but the minute they started to compare themselves with those whose lives were a little more successful, they were brought crashing down to the ground. The best advice would be to seek professional help to get them back on their feet.

"For certain you have to be lost to find something that cannot be found, else everyone would know where it is." Captain Barbossa (Pirates of the Caribbean: At World's End)

That quote speaks volumes. Those who feel they are lost, rest assured that you will always make it out and find something more meaningful to live for. A professional can certainly help you crack the code and get you back on your feet. Before you know it, you will be riding the waves of life once again; only this time, you will be stronger.

There may be some people who might bother you a little more than usual, especially once they see how changed a person you are and how poised you have become to seek your goals. If the issue remains despite friendly warnings, it is best to cut them off. Always aim to be around people who do not judge you and are rather interested to bring the best out in you. Such people cannot just be a blessing but a joy to be around.

Comparing yourself, or anyone else for that matter, with anyone, is nothing less than an evil and vile act. It is a way to make someone feel demotivated and lose their progress. The sooner we understand how badly this affects us and those around us, the sooner we can learn how to say goodbye to it.

Stay true to your cause, and pay attention to your goals. These are nothing more than a part of life, an occurrence that all of us will have to deal with. Do not let words move you away from your goals. The same people who may criticize you today will be the same people to praise you the most once you make it through, and that day, you will genuinely feel victorious.

FINAL TIPS

Before we end this chapter, there are two more things I would like to share with you. These have helped me immensely throughout my recovery and they continue to assist me today in making me a better person.

The first part is quite easy to understand. I wish I had some nicer way to put it but know that we have been brainwashed from day one. It does not take a genius to figure out how easily we fall for false concepts of success and take them to be true.

We are led to believe that success is gauged by a few specific things. However, I am here to tell you that is not the case. Success is not materialistic and sometimes it does not need to be grand either. Small actions that you would carry out in a day can often change someone's life completely.

We have all heard stories of how some of the most successful people found a new purpose that they pursued and eventually made it big, and most of the time that is due to someone's small gestures that moved them.

We exist in a world where people run after praise. The fact is that praise is on a brink of exhaustion, and soon there won't anymore praise to give. Does that mean success would stop? Not at all. Praise, most of the time, is an indication that the person may expect something from you in future. Do not let the amount of praise you get dictate your life. Treat them as background noise and where possible, draw some motivation from them.

We are constantly engaged in a race to win favors, to multitask without actually paying attention to the fact that we may need to slow down a bit and reflect upon how our actions affect us and those around us. Do not be a part of this rat race. This race will only benefit a select few, the rest would just be pawns in a big chess game, ready to be sacrificed and forgotten.

I continue to remind myself of how society works and this has genuinely helped me to wake others up. I have often been asked if people ignore society, who would care for them, and my answer has always been the same; you will care for yourself.

This brings me to the second tip I wish to share with you. While many would come and go in your life, the only one who will be there from the start till the end is your own self. Practice the art of self-love and self-care. This may sound a little awkward but I assure you, this has nothing to do with pleasure.

You need to find ways to encourage yourself when others are clearly hell-bent to make you feel miserable. They may say that you are not good enough, but tell yourself that they do not understand your true capabilities. If you go on to argue with people who are ill-informed or have no prior experience, you would never be able to explain to them how things work. Try not to waste your time ruining your positive vibes and energy defending yourself. Just walk away.

I keep a journal with me where I continue to write all the good acts I have done in the day and the things I am grateful for. Whenever I feel down, it only takes a quick glance to it to immediately feel better. I would recommend keeping such a journal with yourself. Not only would it help you to reflect on your life and all your achievements, but it would also serve as a reminder of why you should always be thankful.

With that said, you have officially learned the five steps which you can work on, master, and apply to dramatically change your life and come out of existence and into life itself. What awaits you is sheer joy, excitement, challenges which you would always learn from, and so much more.

Believe in yourself when no one else is ready to do so. Your life is your story, and how you lead it is only your choice to make. Be wise, be strong, for the journey has just begun!

FINAL WORDS

When you feel you have lost your purpose in life, even the smallest ideas and actions can bring you out of the darkness and into the bright light. The problem is, most have no clue what this idea would be or where to even look for it.

You began your journey as someone who was stressed out, worried and lost. Throughout this book, you have shown a heart that is as strong as I have ever seen. You have shown sheer will and dedication, and you have successfully persevered to ensure you go through the entire book to learn just how you can change your life from this hollow existence and really start living. Let me be the first one to say this:

"Congratulations! You have made it!"

Five easy steps, five life-changing aspects which will forever change the way you think of yourself and of the world. Your life is your unique story. The ups and downs are something we all go through, but what really matters is our ability to rise back up and grab what is rightfully ours.

Throughout this book, we learned how to start thinking positively, how to manage our actions, how to find our purpose, and where to look for our passion. We learned about how important goals are in life and how easily people tend to get them wrong. We figured out the difference between wants and needs, and we created a to-do list that would help us organize our lives a little better. Truly, we have gone through what can only be defined as the most crucial turning point in our lives.

All you need is a spark and the rest is history. I genuinely hope that I was able to contribute to your search for a more meaningful life. Your success is yours to live and cherish, however, owing to my passion, I would love to know about how things changed for you.

Remember your past, live your present, and make your future the best you can. I would love to hear from you on what truly helped you and inspired you to become a better person. **If this has helped you in anyway please leave a review** so I may know how it has. I may not know who you are in person, but I would be surely thrilled to know that I was able to pass on knowledge that went on to change someone's life.

I wish you nothing but the best and I hope that one day, I get to read about you and your success somewhere in the future. Stay strong and believe!

15 QUESTIONS YOU MUST ASK YOURSELF

(OPEN YOUR MIND TO FIND THE OPPORTUNITY)

Don't Stop, Won't Stop

15 QUESTIONS YOU MUST ASK YOURSELF.

www.AlecMoonee.com

These Worksheet Includes:

- 15 Questions you cannot leave unanswered.
- 15 Deep thinking questions to unpack your passion.
- The ability to open your mind.

The last thing we want is you not having the head start to finding your meaning, purpose, passion.

To receive your 15 Question Worksheet, Visit this link (PS. It's Free):

https://tinyurl.com/DontStopWontStop

RESOURCES

Junttila, H. (2013). *Find your passion: 25 questions you must ask yourself.* CreateSpace Independent Publishing Platform.

Martin, L. (2014). *The Difference Between Being Alive And Living: Your Life Should Be More Than Just Breathing.* Elite Daily. https://www.elitedaily.com/life/the-difference-between-being-alive-and-living-your-life-should-be-more-than-just-breathing

SMART Goals: How to Make Your Goals Achievable. (n.d.). Mind Tools. https://www.mindtools.com/pages/article/smart-goals.htm

Spero, H. (n.d.). *How to Determine What Drives You (and Why It's Important).* Shine. https://advice.shinetext.com/

articles/how-to-determine-what-drives-you-and-why-its-important/

Stevenson, J. (2018, September 27). *Here's Why You Keep On Resisting Your Life Purpose.* Medium. https://medium.com/swlh/your-life-purpose-is-staring-you-in-the-face-4-ways-to-recognize-it-5922b16cfb20

The Value of Purpose, Passion, and Vision, and How to Achieve Success. (2019, January 14). Ashford University. https://www.ashford.edu/blog/career-tips/the-value-of-purpose-passion-and-vision-and-how-to-achieve-success

.

Printed in Great Britain
by Amazon